50 PLUS & FABULOUS™

HOW TO LIVE YOUR BEST LIFE

Linda H. Williams

Linda H. Williams

50 PLUS
&
Fabulous

HOW TO LIVE YOUR BEST LIFE

Linda H. Williams

Pearly Gates Publishing, LLC, Houston, Texas (USA)

50 Plus & Fabulous:
How to Live Your Best Life

Copyright © 2021
Linda H. Williams

All Rights Reserved.
No portion of this publication may be reproduced, stored in an electronic system, or transmitted in any form or by any means (electronic, mechanical, photocopy, recording, or otherwise) without written permission from the author or publisher. Brief quotations may be used in literary reviews.

Paperback ISBN 13: 978-1-948853-33-0
Digital ISBN 13: 978-1-948853-34-7
Library of Congress Control Number: 2021919974

Some names and identifying details have been changed to protect the privacy of individuals.

For information and bulk ordering, contact:
Pearly Gates Publishing, LLC
Angela Edwards, CEO
P.O. Box 62287
Houston, TX 77205
BestSeller@PearlyGatesPublishing.com

Linda H. Williams

Giving Thanks

First and foremost, I give honor and thanks to **God Almighty**. Without Him, my *BEST LIFE* would be without meaning.

Thank you always to my Dad and Mom, **Rev. & Mrs. John T. Hilliard**, who showed me what "Living Your Best Life" looks like.

Thank you to my sons, **Emory and Raphael**, who get to see their mom come from where I was to where I am now — "Living My Best Life"! They loved me through the bad times and continue to love me in the good times.

Thank you to my contributors for sharing how they're living their best lives as examples to others *(in order of appearance)*:

- **Melissa A. Secka**
- **Annette Ransom**
- **Karmen Yvette Pratt Moon**
- **Sonya Hanks**
- **Vanessa Austin**
- **Kimberly Holmes Evans**
- **Calvenia Jackson-Bowles**

Living My Best Life…

****

Melissa A. Secka, Age 57

Living Your Best Life…begins with an attitude of gratitude.

God has so richly blessed my life. I am so grateful for my family, my son, and my beautiful grandchildren. After all I've been through, I am still in my right mind. I have the opportunity to start over—not from scratch, but from experience. As my Uncle Aubrey Cumberlander used to say, "You ain't too late, you just late in the game!"

"I am truly 'Living My Best Life'!"

****

Annette Ransom, Age 65

Living Your Best Life…begins with an attitude of gratitude.

I am so grateful that God has given me a loving family and loyal friends. I have so much joy in my heart that God has blessed me with a calling on my life to take care of special needs children. An abundance of love is living your best life…not things.

"This is my blessed and best life!"

****

Karmen Yvette Pratt Moon, Age 55

Living Your Best Life... begins with an attitude of gratitude.

Living my best life is being blessed to have a circle of girlfriends that we can let our hair down and be ourselves. Each one plays a special role and purpose in my life, and I am so thankful for them. I appreciate the love of a good family, good health and strength, and the knowledge that I am preparing for an even better life. God is blessing me every day.

> *"I am blessed to be a blessing to someone else! That's living my best life!"*

****

Sonya Hanks, Age 52

Living Your Best Life... begins with an attitude of gratitude.

I am so grateful that my soul magnifies the Lord. God has allowed me to be around women who are transparent and honest. This provides me with the opportunity to be my authentic self. Living one's best life is always in front of them, never behind. Trust the process. It is never too late to enjoy a group of girlfriends that will take you under their wings and love you for being you. I am thankful that I encountered some special women in Olivet Church. I am living my best life right now with my first-ever group of girlfriends!

> *"My best life can only get better!"*

****

Vanessa Austin, Age 55

Living Your Best Life... begins with an attitude of gratitude.

I'm grateful for having a supporting village of mentors that encourage me to continue to take the next steps in this journey I've been on since 2013. God gave me a little push when I got displaced from the corporate America workforce. And because I have been obedient, God has continued to sustain me in the success of my business, opening opportunities as I continue this journey of growth in my business endeavors.

I have to mention you, Linda, because God placed you in my life at the right time to pour in my spirit and give me confirmation that this is what I'm supposed to be doing.

I continue to look to Him, knowing He will never steer me away from what He has in store.

"Living my best life and being obedient to God's will!"

****

Kimberly Holmes Evans, Age 55

Living Your Best Life... begins with an attitude of gratitude.

From 18 to 23, I had four children in five years by three "baby daddies" who didn't care enough to stay. However, I trusted God through the good and bad times. We grew up together, sharing every victory and defeat, never missing a beat or meal. My babies are now grown and doing well with families of their own. Let our story be an inspiration to you. GOD can take a bad situation and turn it around for good. Keep your head held high, no matter what you may be going through. There's a brighter day ahead!

"God brought me through to live 'my best life!'"

****

Calvenia Jackson-Bowles, Age 55

Living Your Best Life... begins with an attitude of gratitude.

How do you live your best life while battling cancer and helping your husband as he battles COVID and pneumonia, all while continuing to work as a health care provider during a pandemic? In the midst of that, I received that dreaded call from Human Resources: After 27 years of service, my position was being offered to someone else. What a bitter pill to swallow!

I thought I was living large. I had the man, the children, the home on the hill, and people admired me. What did I do to deserve that heartache and pain? I needed answers quickly!

Have you ever been so down that your only way up was to pray? I asked God for answers because I thought He had just forsaken me. My outlets were gone—my health, my church closed. The devil began to live in my idle thoughts. "Wait a minute!" I said to myself. "The devil is a LIAR!"

God stepped in, stopped by my home one night, and said, "I made you to be purposeful, to be a disciple, and to know who to call on in the time of crisis. You have family and friends who love you. This is your opportunity to make this your testimony!" It was time for me to renew my mind and realize that God made me a survivor and a warrior. I was created to praise HIM, no matter what my circumstances.

I am now living my best life. You have to know that when you face life's challenges, it's time to pray and seek guidance. It doesn't matter how low you get because God is a lifter of your head. He will make your burdens light and your yoke easy. When God has been good to you, spread the word of His goodness and greatness. Tell your story to help someone else. That's part of our purpose! God will not leave you, no matter where you make your bed. He is always with you.

When I left my pity-party, I soon became oh so thankful! I had finished my 20 rounds of chemo, and my husband returned to work healthy and strong. I realized the bills were getting paid, despite our situation.

The things I thought were "living" were not as important as LIFE! My best life became living—LIVING through it all. People admire me now for what I have endured, as opposed to what I may have acquired. God is so AWESOME! Trust and believe: We all have our crosses to bear. Some are lighter than mine; some are heavier. This, however, is my testimony.

"Be your best self and live your best life! God Bless!"

Linda H. Williams

Introduction

As we live longer, the images of age and aging are changing throughout the world. The belief that 50 is "middle-aged" no longer holds true. People approaching that golden age have begun to look forward to new beginnings. Furthermore, those in their 60s, 70s, and even 90s are still productive members of society!

We are facing challenges in uncharted waters, including activities such as online dating, raising grandchildren, and more!

While it's true that we are living longer lives, the key to living longer and healthier is in our ability to continue making good decisions. It is undoubtedly true that as we age, we are faced with certain obstacles. However, despite those challenges, we must stay active and productive. We have to believe in our capabilities and not expect to be limited by our age.

How many of you know people who worked 40 or 50 years, only to retire, sit home, "take it easy,"…and then die?

If you stop to think about it, the privilege of growing older is not afforded to everyone. Unfortunately, many of us fail to see aging as a blessing. By the time you have reached your 50s, you have probably lived longer than the years you have left. That is actually a great time to figure out what you want to be "when you grow up"—a time to think about all of those unrealized and forgotten dreams. The uncertainty of your life a decade or two earlier has vanished, and you might actually reach those dreams! In fact, many people find it to be the perfect time to make "new beginnings" in their lives in the pursuit of happiness, health, and overall wellbeing. The problem is that many people do not prepare for their "life after 50." Does it encompass retirement? Widowhood? Something else life-changing? As you can see, life can become an extension of uncertainty because you may find yourself unsure of how to embrace life now.

The process of "reinvention" starts at work, long before you reach the age when you are considered an "elder." You reach a point in your life when outside forces and inner yearnings combine to convince you that you need a new path. The passion for life no longer revolves around your job, and you suddenly realize you don't live for your job. Your employment only provides you with the means to live a life of relative normalcy.

To be vital and relevant, you find yourself searching for your life's purpose. As a result, somewhere in your 50s, you begin to think about what you are passionate about. Therein lies your purpose! A person who waits until retirement to discover their purpose most likely continues to search…and search…and search.

For those of us considered to be "Baby Boomers," life for our parents consisted of working for the same company for 40 or 50 years, retiring with a gold watch and a healthy pension, and then moving to Florida to bask in the sun. Those days are gone. It's unlikely you will receive a gold watch or pension, and basking in the sun all day, every day will likely cause skin cancer!

We have to reinvent ourselves constantly. We don't start from scratch; we start from experience. The process of reinvention often isn't easy. "Change is hard," says Lynn Berger, a New York City career coach. "You have to take the time to understand what is happening, not just feel threatened and react." Our lives become so structured around our work schedule that we become dependent on that very thing to provide our motivation to "DO" anything!

Know this: Reinvention is inevitable in some of the more personal aspects of our lives. As we age, health issues will arise, and ever-changing family dynamics necessitate changes in our relationships with spouses, lovers, children, and parents. As those things happen, we naturally begin to ponder our purpose and values more deeply.

Reinvention isn't just about existing. It's about living, thriving, and making the rest of your life the BEST of your life. It's about relaunching your life in a way that makes you smile.

"The first half of our life is about being interesting," says Chip Conley, author of *Wisdom @ Work: The Making of a Modern Elder*. "The second half is about being interested."

Be Blessed!

Linda H. Williams

Table of Contents

Giving Thanks vi

Living My Best Life… vii

Introduction xii

Chapter 1: Caregiving.. 1

Chapter 2: Being Single 9

Chapter 3: Personal Development.................................... 15

Chapter 4: Dating 22

Chapter 5: Healthy Relationships..................................... 28

Chapter 6: Alone vs. Lonely 36

Chapter 7: Your Finances 44

Chapter 8: Healthy Living 57

Chapter 9: Faith and Forgiveness..................................... 71

Chapter 10: Finding Your Purpose 84

Chapter 11: Scams, Slams, and Flim-Flams 90

Chapter 12: The Sandwich Generation........................... 100

Conclusion 108

About the Author 109

Chapter 1
Caregiving

"There will come a time when your loved one will be gone and you will find comfort in the fact that you were their caregiver."
~ Karen Coetzer ~

When my mom got too sick to take care of herself and knew her time was drawing to a close, she asked if we would please let her transition at home. We all agreed: "Mom, whatever you want."

I had no idea what caregiving involved.

Even as we continue to age, caring for our aging parents can definitely become an overwhelming experience. Caring for our parent(s) is not a job we apply for; it is one that can happen in a split second, such as receiving a call one morning that one of our parents has been diagnosed with a debilitating and possibly terminal illness. Our on-the-job training comes with unbelievable highs and lows, leaving us to feel as if we've been on one of the wildest rollercoaster rides on the planet!

Then, there's the flipside of the same coin. If you are blessed to have an elderly parent who is still physically and mentally alert, that can be another challenge. How often has your parent said, "I might be old, but I'm not dead yet! I'll let you know when I need your help"? My 93-year-old dad says that often. It can be quite challenging as they fight to maintain their independence. It is imperative that as we provide the care they need, we allow them to maintain as much independence as possible.

Certain inevitable changes come with aging. With all of those changes, our parents' independence is one of a few factors over which they have control. It is vital that seniors have a sense of freedom. As with anyone, it gives a sense of purpose, achievement, and self-worth. According to a recent survey, "More people are more afraid of losing their independence as they grow older than of dying." So, in addition to balancing their wants, needs, and best interests, you also need to be mindful of their independence. Be careful not to cross the boundary between caregiving and taking over their lives.

Undoubtedly, that can be stressful, especially when you have no idea the level of responsibility and are without the benefit of prior life experience as a caregiver for aging parents. That is why caregivers are at such high risk for overload and potentially serious health conditions.

So, if you are caring for your older adult at home, it is imperative that you pace yourself. That means you cannot be running at 110% every day. You are human. Overworking yourself is simply not sustainable over the long run. Pacing yourself and getting assistance helps you stay as healthy as possible so that you can continue providing great care. In order to do that, you must recognize some of the challenges you will face.

1. **We have to perform tasks that we never imagined.** Typically, caregiving begins with small, more manageable tasks such as grocery shopping, helping around the house, etc. At this stage, life is relatively simple and can fit into our busy schedules. But, as our parents experience declining health, we may find that our role as a caregiver can become quite stressful. What happens when you need to bathe your parent, change a Depend, or clean a catheter bag? It's a difficult task to discuss with your parent about letting you clean their private parts to keep them from getting infections. We must remember that they have not lost their dignity or self-respect just because they cannot adequately care for themselves. Unfortunately, as our parents age, we sometimes have to take care of some of their basic needs, just as they did for us when we were infants and toddlers. The difference is this: Somewhere deep inside still lives an adult. When we start to treat them as if they are infants, we rob them of their dignity and self-respect.

   So, what to do? Ask for help. Prepare a list of tasks that can be done by someone else. It might be running errands, picking up groceries, sitting for a while so you can take a break, or even cooking a meal. Often, friends are willing and available to help. Don't be afraid to ask.

2. **Family disagreements.** Caregiving is a very difficult and stressful time for all family members, especially siblings.

It is not unusual for decisions regarding who will be the primary caregiver and decision-maker for our parents to dissolve into unexpected battles. A typical scenario is where one sibling takes on the primary role of caregiving, and the siblings offer no support. The latter may feel that the responsibility falls upon the sibling living closest to the parent needing the help. Logistically, that makes sense, but it doesn't lessen the tension caused by the additional responsibility falling on that particular sibling. Out-of-town siblings might "slide" into town for a visit to see mom and dad and can quickly assume the persona of denial because all seems well. What is not understood is that the appearance of "all is well" is only made possible because the default sibling caregiver has taken care of the details. In a perfect situation, all siblings would get along and live within close proximity to their parent(s). Life, though, is not perfect!

So, what to do? Get an external evaluation of your parent's current mental and physical capacity. Make sure all siblings involved are present for the results. That way, everyone will be on the same page regarding the reality of the situation. This is particularly important if siblings live out of town and aren't necessarily able to give physical support. They can, however, provide financial support to perhaps bring in someone else to assist the primary caregiver. Communication is always the key to at least making sure everyone is aware.

3. **Loss of their independence.** Aging parents struggle fiercely to retain some sense of control over their lives

that becomes narrower with time. This becomes increasingly stressful for the caregiver who has to try to be there for them without making them angry for "taking over." During this time, spouses and long-time friends pass away, driving becomes challenging, and their health slowly declines. Life after retirement should be a time to reinvent yourself and finally pursue the passion put on hold so many years ago. Unfortunately, for many, this becomes a life of grief, declining health, and loss. Because we (as adult children) typically have hectic lives, it becomes much easier to take control of the situation and just tell our parents what they should and should not do. Therein lies the struggle—a tug-of-war of sorts. Aging parents are determined to retain their independence, even as we see them failing at some of the most basic tasks. In response, we are committed to making life easy as possible for everyone concerned by taking control. To be totally honest here, it is unfortunate that there is no roadmap on how to deal with this situation that will satisfy everyone. There are no quick solutions to helping aging parents accept that they can no longer perform some of the tasks they may be used to handling. Likewise, there is no perfect way to offer help to someone trying to come to grips with the slow demise of their independence.

So, what to do? While balancing their wants, needs, and what's in their best interest, keep in mind that nobody willingly gives up their independence. The line between caregiving and being overbearing is a thin one and can very easily be crossed. Sometimes, we must put ourselves in their shoes and learn how to communicate with them as the adults they actually are and not the child they may actually display. Giving up the keys to the car is probably the most difficult. The time to discuss their declining driving skills is not when you're in the passenger's seat!

4. **Caregivers often sacrifice friends and social activities to tend to the responsibilities of caregiving.** Life for the caregiver becomes a combination of a teeter-totter, rollercoaster, and merry-go-round, all in one. It can consist of highs and lows, ups and downs, and simply a feeling that you're going around in circles sometimes. Your life suddenly takes a back seat — if not put on hold altogether — while you try to navigate this new and uncharted path that your life has suddenly taken. Where once you may have loved to socialize, go out, or have friends over, you've become so consumed with caring that you find you no longer have the energy to be "the life of the party" you once were. Sometimes, you become so consumed with your caregiver duties and scheduling your life around those tasks that you stop nurturing other relationships and the enjoyment you receive from them. As caregivers, it is essential not to lose focus on the responsibilities of taking care of ourselves. If we don't provide ourselves healthy outlets to recover both mentally and physically, we can easily become overwhelmed and overworked! Every now and then, we must hit that pause button to maintain healthy social ties (even if it's a short-term distraction) and find someone to talk to and laugh with.

So, what to do? While it may be difficult during this time to allow friends "into your world," it is essential that you do. There is no reason to feel guilty about taking a friend's offer to help you. They offer because they care. Even if you can't go out or speak to your friends as often, let them know you appreciate them but may not have the time right then. Set aside a specific time to either talk to friends or perhaps schedule a social outing. You may be able to actually have a few friends over for an in-house lunch date. If you find yourself constantly saying, "We should get together sometime," with no real plan to do so, those friends will quickly fall off your radar.

5. **There is no roadmap to aging or caregiving!** Just like there is no other way to learn to care for your newborn baby other than just doing it, so it is with growing older and caring for aging parents. It's more than a shock to realize that Medicare doesn't cover all the costs associated with aging. Who knew that you have to pay for in-home care or that your parents can have no assets in order to qualify for assisted living through Medicaid? It can become quite frustrating that medical appointments may last only 15 minutes or that prescriptions are written with no explanation. Hence, you find yourself trying to do what's best when you have little to no information about what anything outside of your "normal" looks like. (It can be a blessing to have a family member in the healthcare field.) Regardless, you have to stay on top of your family member's healthcare needs.

So, what to do? Ask questions! Why are they taking this medication? Research the uses and side effects of all medicines. It may be that some of the symptoms displayed are a result of interactions from various medications. Google is a powerful tool. Use it as a tool to gather information to stay informed. Stay on top of your healthcare providers. Trust me: The more you are on top of your loved one's care and treatment, the better the treatment. Remember: "The squeaky wheel gets the grease!" You don't want to be rude or annoying, though. Those people are the ones taking care of your parents. It's like angering the person serving your food. That's never a good idea!

Taking care of our elderly parents comes from a place of love. Love alone is not enough, though. You must be prepared and knowledgeable to have the confidence to handle the situation. It's important to recognize that your loved one will never be like they used to be. Acceptance of their current circumstance goes a long way in diffusing conflict, ultimately leading to a more cohesive union.

Living Your Best Life!

Chapter 2
Being Single

"Being single means you're strong enough to wait for what you deserve."
~ Niall Horan ~

There are many reasons for being single. It can be a result of never marrying, once married-now divorced, or the loss of your loved one. Whatever the reason, it's a lifestyle that can be embraced and enjoyed or looked upon as a sentence to be endured. Being single has often been stereotyped and stigmatized. Until the "Baby Boomer" generation, being single and happy after 50 was almost unheard of. But if you were to actually take a look at how people truly feel and how the outside world assumes they feel, you might find a totally different picture.

Over time, being single should get better, and thus, self-satisfaction should also get better. Where once, not having a partner signaled loneliness, being single now opens up a brand-new world of possibilities!

If you look back over the span of your life, you will see how in your teens, you waited by the phone (which was usually attached to the kitchen wall) for it to ring. In your 20s, you thought you were grown and knew everything, only to find out the path you took led to broken hearts and broken relationships. The 30s brought on a fear that your biological clock was ticking and that you needed to hurry up. So, of course, your 40s dealt with the consequences of bad decisions made in your 30s, such as divorce, single parenting, etc. Your 50s should be a time devoted to rediscovering or, in some cases, discovering yourself.

Let's be clear: Being single and happy in your 50s is not automatic. It doesn't happen "just because." It takes courage, especially if many of your peers are into their 3rd or 4th decade of marriage. If you're not careful, the "would'ves, could'ves, and should'ves" will set in. You will begin to reflect on certain decisions you made and question whether they were the right ones. Know that whatever the choice made to get you to this place in your life was the right one for that time. Monday morning quarterbacks always win the game!

So, how do you enjoy the single life at 50 plus?

1. **Get to know yourself.** If you are comfortable with yourself, your marital status has no bearing on the quality of your life. Sometimes, we get "lost" in relationships and wonder why we're not happy. We spend so much time taking care of others and getting to know them that we either forget or run out of time to do the same for ourselves. It's imperative that you discover what you like and don't like so that you can establish boundaries for yourself and others in your life. Identify your good, bad, and ugly. Everyone has ugly! This gives

you a starting point and a roadmap with which to begin the process of getting to know the "real" you. We are all aware of the person society or even our families want us to be. Still, unless we know our core values, beliefs, and desires, it will be almost impossible for us to choose a life path and relationships that make us feel happy and fulfilled.

2. **Let go of your past.** You will never enjoy where you are now if you are constantly reliving your past. We all have a past. We all have made bad choices and decisions that ultimately affect our lives. Getting past your past can be a tricky thing. The person you are today is a direct result of your past triumphs, mistakes, and good and bad decisions. It has molded you into the person you have become. If your past is laden with difficult and painful experiences that you cannot get past, cutting yourself off might be easier said than done. Sometimes, you can get stuck and begin to believe that your journey has become your destination. If you are stuck in your past, that can lead to an unhappy present and dismal future. You have baggage, and I have baggage. We all have baggage that we bring with us. It is how you carry that baggage and what you do with it that determines whether it propels you to greater heights or weighs you down.

3. **Learn from what worked and what didn't work.** One thing is for sure: Life is about lessons. Unless you learn from the lesson, you will continue to make the same mistakes. Formal education is all about learning the lesson and then taking a test. Life is about the test and

then learning the lesson! It is not all about the other person, either. We sometimes become so focused on what someone else did or did not do that we neglect to acknowledge our role. For example, when I lost my home, I blamed someone else—until I realized I had stopped making the mortgage payments because I depended on someone else. I had to accept that I lost my home because I stopped taking care of MY business! Our growth comes from self-examination. It is healthy to examine past relationships and experiences to ensure you don't make the same mistakes. Your past holds some of your greatest treasures to better equip you for your future. It also holds some of your greatest challenges that may be preventing you from becoming all you were created to be. Your keys to a happy and successful life now depend on your ability to learn what your past has taught you. Forgive those who have hurt you—including yourself—and allow your past to be your history, not your sentence.

4. **Be about the business of you.** With society placing so much emphasis on being in a relationship, women often spend way too much time concentrating on finding a man. Unfortunately, our generation was taught that we needed a man to complete us. Thusly, without one, we tend to feel inadequate. Nothing could be further from the truth. Instead of worrying about finding a man, try filling your life with things that make you happy and people who make you laugh. I'm reminded of Mrs. Noah. She took care of everybody and every animal on the ark, and when the ark landed and everyone went

their own way, Mrs. Noah was left with nothing to do (or so it seemed). You see, it was finally time that she could focus on herself! Unfortunately, we never get to know if she accomplished her goals because she is never mentioned in the Bible again. How unfortunate is it to spend our entire lives thinking about and catering to others, all while neglecting ourselves? Now is your time! What do you want to be when you grow up? What are you passionate about? Your purpose lies within your passion.

5. **Establish an independent routine.** Embrace the fact that you can do what you want, when you want, and with whom you want with no restrictions. That is a luxury not everyone can enjoy! As a "single," you can come and go as you please without explanation. You can travel to places you've always wanted to or just simply have a relaxing evening without interruptions. Since you are in control of your schedule, you can establish a routine that works for you. Are you more productive in the morning? Do you want to start your day exercising, meditating, or writing in your journal? Do whatever pleases you! It's important, though, to establish a routine. Otherwise, you can spend countless mindless, unproductive days in front of the television or (worse yet) playing games on your phone or tablet.

6. **Begin to do things by yourself.** How many times have you said or heard, "The more, the merrier"? While doing things with others may improve our mental and physical state and bring us happiness and laughter, it is

also important to do things on our own. The only way to know if you like the person you are alone with when you are by yourself is to spend time by yourself! The very act of doing something on your own means you must rely solely on yourself without any input from another. That means whatever decision you make and the resulting consequence rest solely on your shoulders, thus eliminating the possibility of you placing blame on someone else. You have to face whatever the situation is and figure it out by yourself. Spending quality time by yourself makes you believe in yourself, thereby increasing your self-confidence and self-esteem. A healthy balance in life requires spending time with others and spending time with yourself.

Society needs to become more sophisticated in how they think about people who do not have romantic partners, rather than just lumping everyone together, regardless of whether they are widowed, divorced, separated, or have been single their whole life. It is probably still a surprise to many that lifelong single people are often happier and doing the best!

Living Your Best Life!

Chapter 3
Personal Development

"It is never too late to be who you might have been."
~ George Eliot ~

Personal growth and development has been defined as a transformational process in which improvements are made in your physical, emotional, intellectual, spiritual, social, and/or financial state. In this chapter, we will concentrate on your emotional and intellectual growth. The other areas will be discussed in upcoming chapters.

It is a proven fact that our emotional and intellectual wellbeing hinges on several factors in our life. Let's look at some of them.

1. **Self-Confidence.** Confidence is described as "a feeling of self-assurance arising from one's appreciation of one's abilities or qualities." Some people seem to be dripping with it, while others seem to have to search everywhere just to find a nugget! Having confidence in yourself is essential to living a happy, full, and productive life. Even those who seem to have a high level of confidence will, at some point, ride the highs and lows of the

confidence rollercoaster. Adverse events in your life can send your confidence and self-esteem spiraling down a slippery slope. Ill health, job loss, a general feeling of lack of control, and unfulfilling relationships can cause an otherwise confident person to become withdrawn into themselves. It is important to remember that what we feed our minds directly correlates to what is manifested in our lives. What we say to ourselves about ourselves will eventually begin to take root and actually become that very thing. So, how do we boost our confidence and self-esteem?

    a. **Eliminate your inner critic.** Have you ever listened to the conversations you have with yourself about yourself? How many times have you asked, "How could I have been so stupid?" or "I can't believe I've gotten myself in this same situation again! What is wrong with me?!" We all talk to ourselves, whether aloud or in the confines of our heads. When those conversations happen, we listen to them. If you speak negatively about yourself often enough, you will begin to believe that negativity. In response, your actions begin to manifest that belief, even if on an intellectual level, you know the negative things you say to yourself are not true. Begin to listen to what you are saying to yourself. Replace "I can't" and "I'm not" with "I can" and "I am." That's a start! Think of everything you have to be grateful for.

b. **Cultivate an attitude of gratitude.** Do you make it a habit of being thankful and appreciative of what you have? Or do you concentrate on what you don't have or wish you had? Oprah says, "Be thankful for what you have; you'll end up having more. If you concentrate on what you don't have, you'll never, ever have enough." It can be quite difficult to see, much less concentrate on what is good in your life when there seems to be so much that is not. You think about where you are and where you could be if things had worked out differently, and we find ourselves going down "IF ONLY ROAD." We all have situations and decisions we have made in the past that, if we could redo, we would consider a different choice. However, the fact is we are where we are. If we think for a minute and are honest with ourselves, we know things could be a whole lot worse. Try starting a gratitude journal. Every day, think of one thing you are grateful for or one positive thing in your life. Then, every time you start to feel sorry for yourself, pull out your journal and focus on the good things in your life.

2. **Accepting responsibility.** Accepting responsibility for the actions in our life is probably one of the most important aspects of personal development. It is fairly easy to be gracious and accept success in good times, but it takes a strong character to successfully cope with the adversities of life—those failures we come in contact with...the bumps in the road that we will inevitably

meet on life's journey, yet still move forward with a positive attitude. Not accepting responsibility for ourselves and our actions will cause us to have low self-esteem. By blaming someone else, we have permitted that person to determine our self-worth. We must stop saying, "It's not my fault," or "I didn't have the best upbringing," or "Something bad happened to me as a child." They are all excuses we use to refuse accepting responsibility for ourselves. Yes, things may have happened in our lives, but that was "yesterday." If we are still making choices based on yesterday's things that we cannot go back and change, then we have to accept responsibility for the consequences. How do we begin to accept responsibility for ourselves?

    a. **Stop blaming others.** You have to stop blaming other people. Everybody has someone they could blame for something that happened in their life, but the reality of life is that you make choices, and those choices have consequences. Where you are today is the result of a decision you made yesterday. So, if you want your tomorrow to be different, you must make better decisions to make those necessary changes. Stop saying it is someone else's fault for those situations in which you find yourself.

    b. **Stop playing the victim.** When you don't accept responsibility, you place yourself in the role of victim. Whether you realize it or not, you are saying, "This is not my fault. Why is this happening to me?" Next thing you know, you are smack dab in the mindset of "Woe is me!" When that happens, you have allowed yourself to play the victim. You sit around doing nothing, waiting for someone to come along and rescue you. Then, once you allow that rescue, you are following their path for your life. That just furthers your victim mentality. To be an overcomer, you must go from a victim mentality to that of a survivor. Say aloud, "I am not a victim! I will have a say-so in my destiny!"

c. **Be accountable.** We have to accept that we are solely responsible for our actions and subsequent consequence. No matter the situation, we ultimately make a choice on how we are going to respond. We may not be able to control the person or situation, but we have control over ourselves. Even if we don't respond, we've made a decision not to and have allowed someone else to make that decision for us. We can blame others, make excuses, whine, or do whatever else, but we must take some positive steps to effect change at the end of the day. If something is going on in your life that you don't like, change it. If something is broken in your life, fix it. Small changes can lead to big results!

3. **Improving your skills.** We never get too old to learn. Once you get to a point where you don't feel you can learn anything from anyone, you have become useless to

yourself and others. This should be the time in your life when you finally have the time to really think about what you want to be when you grow up—and then pursue it! What dreams did you put on hold to raise your family, support your spouse, and be the "perfect" parent to your children? Now is the time to dust off the "What do I want to be when I grow up?" list. Some of the life lessons and skills you have acquired along your life's journey will actually aid you in determining how you want to live and learn going forward. The adage, "You can't teach an old dog new tricks," actually doesn't have anything to do with age. It is more adapted to a mindset that has become used to doing things a certain way with an unwillingness to adapt to change. How can you improve your skills at this stage in life?

a. **The first thing you must do is a self-assessment.** Whether you're still working towards retirement or have already retired, you have to determine what your lane is NOT. It is very easy to follow someone else's path and go down their rabbit hole if we haven't taken the time to discover our own. What are your strengths and weaknesses? What types of things or projects excite you? What would you do, even if you weren't getting paid to do it?

b. **Set goals.** Based on your self-assessment, you should be able to set goals to begin charting your path. Do some research on S.M.A.R.T. goal setting

— **S**pecific, **M**easurable, **A**ttainable, **R**elevant, and **T**ime-bound.

c. **Write down the types of jobs you think you would be interested in that are based on your self-assessment and S.M.A.R.T. goals worksheet.** Identify what you need to do to reach your goals and what obstacles might prevent you from attaining them.

One of the major components of personal development is your willingness to learn new things. Keep your mind open to the fact that just because we've always believed certain things or done things a certain way, it is the only and best way. As time goes on, we should evolve into someone better than we were yesterday. Learn, grow, and evolve into the person you were meant to be.

Living Your Best Life!

Chapter 4
Dating

"Have enough courage to trust love one more time and always one more time."
~ Maya Angelou ~

Do you remember when dating began with an introduction by a mutual friend? Unfortunately, dating in your 50s and beyond has become a much more complicated thing than those idyllic times of our youth. You might be re-emerging on the dating scene after being out of it for some time. Perhaps you've just become widowed or divorced and suddenly find that you still want the companionship you've grown accustomed to. You set your mind to finding that "someone," only to find that the rules and technology (which didn't exist when you dated before) have changed, and you are clueless on how to play the new game called "Dating in this New Age"! A recent survey indicates that less than 20% of people who are 50 PLUS are actually dating, while 40% said they have considered it but are not actually doing it. Why is it a choice not to date?

1. **Everyone has baggage they bring to the table.** By the time we get to our 50s, we have been around the block a time or two. And with that, we have baggage—both

good and bad—that we carry with us from that time forward. The problem comes when we don't release the old baggage and continue to add new. It doesn't matter if you call it "baggage" or "experience," those past relationships impact your dating life as you age. Unfortunately, we tend to bring the past into our relationships and our conversations. There is nothing worse than trying to deal with ghosts from the past!

2. **As we age, it becomes increasingly more difficult to compromise.** When you are younger, compromise becomes a part of your daily life. You compromise for your children, parents, siblings, job, etc. By the time you reach your 50s, you have developed set patterns of behavior. Your values, goals, and idea of how your life should be are at the head of the table, making it more challenging to accommodate someone else. You will not be growing up together. Instead, you will be grown up and trying to fit with someone. Finding someone who fits is even more challenging. Compromising is about knowing what is important to you, identifying your partner's wants, and finding that middle ground. That is the key to success.

3. **Less patience.** In our younger years, we were more adaptable to going along with someone else's way of doing things. Certified relationship expert, Claire Barber, says, "A major reason why dating in your 50s is so hard is because we have become more set in our ways. This isn't necessarily a bad thing. It just means that it can be harder to get into the flow of dating because you have

less patience for people you don't vibe with." As we age, we also have less patience with insecurity and the whole "getting to know you and your motives" process. If you want to participate in the art of dating in your 50s, you have to learn to be more adaptive. Set a standard of expectation, but don't become so rigid that you are unwilling or unable to re-evaluate.

4. **The dreaded technology.** Technology has become a way of life in these times. Whether it's dating, research, conversation, or whatever, you cannot live your best life and not embrace technology. To that end, it is not unusual to find people 50 and over who do not have a computer, do not want one, and do not know how to use one! The dating rules have changed since we dated "way back then," and you have to learn the new rules. If you are afraid of technology, you will find it a lot more challenging in this new-age dating scene.

5. **Out of practice.** There are many reasons why you may have been out of the dating scene for quite some time. Whatever the reason, you not only might feel out of practice but, more importantly, you might be entering a totally different dating landscape than the one you left! It doesn't matter how long it's been since you went on your last date. Dating again should never be to fill a gap left by the previous relationship. Nor should you date someone trying to fill that void. Your goal should be to enhance your life, not make a life (which we so often try to do). Learn to live with yourself and love yourself first.

That way, you won't be looking for love in all the wrong places.

Dating as a 50 PLUS means taking control of your love life, just as you should in every other aspect of your life. It means knowing yourself. It means being kind to yourself and the men/women you meet. It means making good decisions. Even though some of the rules of dating have changed, the rules of human nature have not. If you don't control your life, including your love life, you allow someone else to step in and take charge. So, what is the key to successful, mature dating? Surely, there has to be something to make dating not just possible but attainable!

1. **Don't make baggage—theirs or yours—the bonding agent.** Everyone has baggage. If you are looking for someone to dump on, get a therapist or life coach. Your date is not the place to relieve yourself of unwanted thoughts, feelings, or emotions. Questions like, "What happened with your marriage/relationship?" or "How has online dating worked for you?" may sound innocent but can lead down a path of negativity. Those questions don't matter if you are looking towards the future and what it might be!

2. **Who calls who?** Our generation was taught that women wait on the man to call to be asked out on a date. The same applied to being asked to dance, which is okay…if you like sitting around and waiting. In today's times, if you enjoyed the date and want to see if it will go further, I suggest you exchange numbers. There is nothing worse

than waiting for someone to call you when you want to talk to them. However, exercise prudence. Ladies, if you call him and leave a voice message, don't call again. If he is interested, he will call you back. If he doesn't, keep it moving. Don't be a desperate, hounding woman!

3. **Are you ready to have a relationship or just sex?** You can get sex from anybody. Trust me: It is just as easy for a woman to find sex as it is for a man. But at your age, do you want to wake up in the morning with flashbacks of your 20s, when you are left wondering why you ever decided to have sex with that man/that woman? This is not the age where you can get a shot or take medication to get rid of something you may have contracted from your partner. There are more than physical maladies that are transmitted through bodily fluids. Unless you are comfortable having a conversation about safe sex and how it affects your relationship afterward, you might want to give careful consideration to your decision. Let your partner know your needs, wants, and feelings. If you are dealing with a mature individual, they will respect you. If not, keep it moving!

4. **Control yourself.** That means presenting yourself in a manner that lets your partner know you are your own woman/man. Ladies, don't be needy or whiney. If you are, you will attract a needy, whiney man (and vice-versa). Now, if that's what you want, go for it! However, if you want a man who is about his business, you have to be about yours. I always say that water seeks its own level. You attract that which you are. A man should

never complete you, only complement you. If you are looking for someone to make you into what you think you should be, try looking in the mirror. That is where you will find that person. If the conversation or his actions make you feel uncomfortable, speak up. You must have standards regarding what you will and will not allow in your space. If you have yet to determine what they are, that is where you need to start before you try dating again.

Remember: Even if they are not Mr./Mrs. Right or Mr./Mrs. Right Now, there is a valuable lesson to be learned from each date. Learn the lesson and move on.

Living Your Best Life!

Chapter 5
Healthy Relationships

"A healthy relationship is a feast of affection/giving for both people; not one receiving crumbs and trying to convince themselves it's enough."
~ Shannon Thomas ~

Even before the pandemic of 2020, the whole concept and definition of relationships had changed. We went from in-person communication to online social media, texting, and pictures to convey our messages. But, at the end of the day, we are sociable creatures, and we need healthy relationships to live our best lives.

When you think about it, there is nothing more valuable than friendships. Consider for a moment those friends in your life who have withstood the test of time, supported you when you were down, loved you when you were up, and stood by you whether you were broke or loaded. Although having a healthy relationship with your friends is important, it is equally important and necessary to have a healthy relationship with your family and yourself. Sometimes, we need our friends. Other times, we need our family. Then, there are the times we just have to know that we will show up for ourselves.

Additionally, since we are spiritual beings encased in a physical body, we must have a healthy relationship with our Creator (this, too, will be discussed in a later chapter).

We were not created to be isolated beings. Healthy relationships are vital to living your best life for the rest of your life!

1. **Friends.** The older we become, the more difficult it is to make new friends. We don't have the time nor the desire to cultivate new relationships. So, the friends we do have, we come to cherish those relationships. While our significant other may play an important part in our lives as we grow older, friendships can ultimately hold the key to our happiness. Our friendships after 50 look very different from those we established in our 20s and 30s. For the 50 PLUS, friendships tend to be more precious and, like anything else worth having, takes time and effort to maintain — although not everyone in your circle will occupy the same space in your life. Aristotle determined there are three types of friends:

    a. **Friendships of utility.** These are people you are on friendly terms with, mainly due to the benefits each of you brings to the table. Examples are business partners, colleagues, schoolmates, and possibly your neighbor.

    b. **Friendships of pleasure.** These are the people you enjoy being in their company…just because. Often, they are the ones you enjoy doing activities with, such as traveling or going to the movies, dinner, or theater—the kind of people you joke around with or enjoy having a conversation with. NOTE: Pleasure comes in many different forms, some of which are not sexual.

c. **Friendships of the good.** These friendships are based on mutual respect and admiration and take longer to build. This comes from a place of discovering similar views, goals, and visions on how things should be. Often, these friendships begin in childhood, adolescence, or college. Thus, they have sustained the test of time.

While we all have people who fit into one of the three categories of friendship, the best is, of course, the "good" ones. Because of the time and effort involved, it is rare (but not impossible) to form good relationships later in life, but in order to have a friend, you must be a friend. How does that happen?

d. **Support, trust, and honesty.** Everybody needs a support system. If you become a frequent no-show when needed, your value decreases. If you fail to show up, you should not be surprised when no one shows up to support you. Can you be trusted? If you cannot be trusted not to speak untruths, spread lies, or gossip, you are not a "good" friend. Without trust, there is no authenticity in the friendship.

e. **Listen and not judge.** We can become so consumed with our own lives that often, we only "half-listen" to what someone is saying to us. However, sustaining a friendship requires attention. If we do not know what our friend needs or state our needs, the friendship will not survive. We must be careful not to judge while listening to our friends. Sometimes, all our friend needs is a sounding board—someone to vent to. It is important not to judge our friends' choices just because they differ from what we think is best for them.

2. **Family.** Healthy family relationships, although desirable, are not always attainable to live your best life. Family should be able to be trusted for support, love, and affection. Family members should feel connected to one another. Sometimes, these relationships involve conflict, which is a normal part of family life. Conflict can occur between adults, children, and young people. Unresolved conflict with your family can greatly diminish your capacity to live your best life. As much as you may say, "It doesn't bother me," if you are truthful with yourself, somewhere deep in your soul, you wish things could be better. Do you ever find yourself admiring or even being jealous of a friend who has a good family bond? Good relationships, especially with your family, is a process and something that must be nourished and fed constantly. Why do family relationships break down?

a. **Inadequate financial planning.** Let's be real: Even a tight-knit family can fall completely apart over money. The first generation acquires money, the second generation may or may not enhance it, and by the third generation, there is usually not enough left to squabble over what remains in the legacy. Solid financial planning and estate planning must be established. Everything should be spelled out in legal documents so that there is no misunderstanding. Who gets what? How is everything to be decided and divided among the heirs? Believe it or not, the people with the least amount usually have the most drama when it comes to family money and heirlooms. The more children, the greater the problems. Write it down! A good idea is to discuss these matters with each sibling and your parents while everyone is still healthy and in their right mind. There may be some things that have changed, and the wills and power of attorneys may need to be updated.

b. **Ineffective communication.** Oftentimes, the patriarch or matriarch of the family leads by instructing everyone on what to do. This may work on young children but does not lend itself to healthy adult sibling communication. As parents, we dictate the relationship we have with our children. If it were left up to the child, they would be best buddies with their parents, treating them as equals. We all know that does not lend itself to a healthy relationship. On the other hand, a strict, no-nonsense, I-am-the-parent/you-are-the-child type of relationship also does not make for the best relationship. We have to learn that the art of communication does not just involve talking; listening is even more critical. Listen to our children, siblings, and older parents. Do not just hear what is being said; also try to understand the feelings behind the words. We grew up in an era where parents were not friends with their children. We could not discuss subjects that made our parents uncomfortable and were deemed inappropriate for a child. I vowed that I would be a parent and a friend to my children. Although that sometimes put our relationship in a gray area, I had no problem bringing it back into focus. Likewise, as children, we were punished for fighting each other but rewarded for having each other's back. Familial relationships must be cultivated and nurtured.

3. **Yourself.** It is impossible to live your best life without having a good relationship with others. It is also impossible to have good relationships with others if you do not have a good relationship with yourself. Everything begins with you. Even airline personnel instruct you to put on your oxygen mask first before assisting others. So, what does a healthy relationship with yourself look like?

   a. **You must value yourself as a person, recognizing your strengths and weaknesses, as**

well as your good, bad, and ugly. Once you recognize these within yourself, you must be careful not to compare yourself to others. We compare our insides to someone else's outside because we only see what someone else is willing to share. Unless you have viewed life as they do and experienced what they have, you are comparing yourself to inaccurate information. Instead, shift your focus and concentrate on what is good in your life. Start to appreciate your gifts, talents, and the uniqueness you bring to the table.

b. **Set boundaries.** You have to set boundaries and limits for yourself in order for you to understand and recognize when someone has crossed the line. When you establish acceptable behaviors or boundaries, you create certain freedoms for yourself because your wishes have been clearly defined. Setting boundaries reflects your self-esteem and values. It says, "I will not tolerate anything that goes against what I believe in!" It teaches others how you expect to be treated and, when that occasional person attempts to challenge that, you simply take root and stand firmly. Oftentimes, we compromise our values for the sake of someone else that ultimately leaves us feeling angry with ourselves while asking, "Why did I do that?!"

c. **Learn how to say, "NO!"** Why is it so difficult for us to say no? We will consent to do something that we either do not want to do or know is wrong in our hearts. Then, we punish ourselves into thinking we have no backbone, which leads us to think we are just a weakling. That is not a healthy view of ourselves and can bring us into a vicious cycle of self-loathing. We can get so used to saying yes and pleasing others that we don't even recognize what we want or need. If your life is so wrapped up in satisfying what other people want that you have lost sight of what is important to you, it is time to make some changes in your decision-making. Saying no can be difficult, but it is a healthy alternative to saying yes and going against your values and moral judgment. Think about all the time, money, and effort you have spent saying yes to things you really should have said no to. This should get you angry enough to spark a flicker of change. Just say, "NO!"

Everything in our lives begins with us and filters out to others. The relationships we have with others are a direct reflection of the relationship we have with ourselves. There is nothing more valuable than having healthy relationships with people you interact with, including yourself. It can be difficult at this point in your life to find the time or energy to create new friendships or to invest in your existing relationships to make them stronger. However, it is a worthwhile investment that can yield powerful results that can strengthen many aspects of your life as well as the lives of others.

Living Your Best Life!

Chapter 6
Alone vs. Lonely

"Loneliness expresses the pain of being alone and solitude expresses the glory of being alone."
~ Paul Tillich ~

Have you ever been happy just to be by yourself? Have there been times when you have been by yourself but wished you had some company? That is the flipside of the same coin. In both instances, you find yourself by yourself, but in only one do you feel lonely. Being alone simply describes a state of solitude when you are outside the company of others. Lonely, on the other hand, represents a state or feeling of abandonment and sadness.

Today, more than any other time in history, women 50 and over live alone — and it is far from a negative experience. Instead, it is liberating and incredibly enriching! Many of us have never lived alone. I was close to 60 before I had my first experience of living alone. I came from a childhood household full of family — mom, dad, siblings, grandparents, aunts, uncles, then to college roomies, husbands, and children of my own.

I remember my best friend, Rosalyn, was an only child. I used to love going to her house because it was quiet and she had her own room (I shared a room with my grandmother). My BFF, on the other hand, although not a lonely child, loved to come to my house because there were so many people, so much noise, and constant activity. I can remember sometimes feeling all alone amid all those people in my home.

No matter what your childhood experiences were of being alone or lonely, it is a good possibility that you may be by yourself at some point in your life.

So, what are some of the differences between loneliness and being alone?

Loneliness is crying without being seen. Being alone is being so consumed with oneself that you smile or laugh for no reason.

Loneliness is the sense of emotional abandon. Being alone is physical and mental freedom.

Loneliness makes you want to find distractions to free yourself from it. Being alone allows you to follow your heart.

Loneliness stems from blaming oneself. Being alone comes from loving oneself.

Loneliness is the feeling of being disconnected. Being alone is connecting with oneself.

Loneliness is the riot in your brain that nobody can hear. Being alone is the quiet everyone can feel.

Loneliness is depending on someone else for happiness. Being alone is finding your own happiness.

Loneliness is longing for something that does not exist. Being alone is enjoying everything that exists in solitude.

Loneliness is rooted in fear. Being alone is rooted in peace.

Loneliness is being restless all the time. Being alone is being content with yourself.

We may all find ourselves in any or all of those emotional dwellings at certain points in our lives. The point is not that we visit them; the problem is taking up residence in the loneliness dwelling! Being okay with being by ourselves is an aspect of emotional growth and knowledge of ourselves. In order to cultivate a more grounded outlook on life as a result of introspection requires you to spend some alone time with your thoughts, ideas, dreams, and frustrations.

The person we present in social gatherings is not our most authentic self. Everyone lives behind a window shade that is only lifted so high, allowing others into our innermost selves. We care about how others perceive us and thus, are influenced by other people's opinions. That can easily set us up to mold ourselves into what others want us to be or what others think. Being what others want us to be may not coincide with the vision of what we want ourselves to be. Consequently, being alone for some introspection is not going to be a happy time. Conversely, filling up empty spaces in our lives with meaningless people or stuff can be even worse! Robin Williams once said, "I used to think the worst thing in life was to end up all alone. It's not. The worst thing in life is to end up with people who make you feel all alone!"

I have discovered that life is so much better when you are by yourself if you like the person you are alone with. One of the greatest joys in life is not finding yourself but liking the person you find. How do you learn to like yourself?

1. **Enjoy your accomplishments.** There is no such thing as an overnight success. Sometimes, you can become so immersed in the journey to success that you fail to celebrate the small, inch-by-inch accomplishments along the way. That usually takes years of hard work in addition to:

    a. **Confidence.** Your achievements—both great and small—should build you up and help you believe that you can accomplish the next goal in front of you.

    b. **Belief.** You must have the belief in your abilities to accomplish your goals. Surround yourself with people who also believe in you. If you are an eagle, soar with the eagles. Do not trudge along with turtles!

    c. **Commitment.** Along with the belief in yourself and your goals, you must be committed. Commitment is proven in your ability to continue again…and again…and again. Celebrating small accomplishments gives you the strength to continue.

   d. **Consistency.** Greatness does not come from doing a big thing once. It is the consistency of doing something every day that leads to the success of your project. You must have the same focus, energy, and purpose consistently on a daily basis to make success possible.

2. **Think about your past but do not dwell on the things you regret.** Everyone has something in their past they wish they could go back and change. We have all made bad choices that sometimes follow us for the rest of our lives. Your past should be a platform from which you have experienced, learned, and became a better person—not a hammer with which you beat yourself up for the rest of your life. Let go of your past:

   a. **Guilt.** Guilt is a normal emotion that lets us know we have done something against our moral fiber and good judgment. It is not meant to be a club with which we continue to beat ourselves up for the rest of our lives. Realize you cannot go back and change the past. You have to interrupt those negative thoughts of what you "should've" or "could've" done differently. Learn from those mistakes, bad choices, and unhealthy situations of the past and move forward.

b. **Accept responsibility.** As humans, it is difficult for us to accept responsibility for our actions. It is much easier to blame someone else and play the victim. When we play the victim, we say, "The reason I am in this situation is not my fault, so it is not my responsibility to get myself out of it!" Once you accept whatever your role was/is, whether minor or major, you can begin to take the necessary steps toward a better life.

c. **Forgiveness.** If we forgive someone for hurting us, we think that we are saying it didn't matter or it was okay. Neither of those is correct. Forgiveness doesn't have anything to do with the other person. Nor does it minimize the hurt or absolve anyone for what they did. Forgiveness is purely a selfish act of cleansing your spirit so that the person no longer has any control over your emotions and, thus, your life. It clears the way for you to begin the process of forgiving yourself.

3. **Be aware of the conversations you have with yourself about yourself.** Do you realize we talk to ourselves 24/7? Even when we are asleep, we talk to ourselves. That is why we sometimes wonder if something actually happened or if we just dreamt it. Whatever you are saying to yourself about yourself, you will eventually begin to believe it. If you are constantly putting yourself down, doubting yourself, and thinking unhealthy thoughts about yourself, you will start to manifest those behavior traits. We all know if someone tells a lie often

enough, they will begin to believe the lie! Start speaking life into your thoughts. Turn negative thoughts into positive ones. Everyone has something good about themselves. Begin to concentrate on what is good in your life.

4. **Make time to do things you actually enjoy doing, not what someone else wants you to do.** We can spend our entire lives taking care of others and totally forget about ourselves. Then, suddenly, everyone we have taken care of has moved on, leaving us feeling empty because our entire purpose for living has vanished. Our children grow up, and our significant other is either gone or developed other interests to keep them busy. We then find ourselves alone…and maybe even lonely. Sit down and reflect on your life. What makes you happy? What would you do, even if you weren't getting paid? That is your passion, and your purpose lies within your passion. If taking care of others makes you happy, find someone to care for. Many people—both seniors and children—desperately want someone to care about them.

"Alone" and "lonely" are often used interchangeably but have two very distinct meanings. To be alone is a state of being, while being lonely is an emotional response to one's condition. In an article published in *Psychology Today* by Dr. Abigail Brenner, "The Importance of Being Alone," Brenner writes, "Being alone allows you to drop your 'social guard,' thus giving you the freedom to be introspective, to think for yourself. You may be able to make better choices and decisions about who you are and what you want without outside influence."

Being alone does not mean being lonely. Use your "alone" time to get to know yourself—your good, bad, and ugly! The more you love yourself, the more you can be more "intentional" about the love you share with others.

Living Your Best Life!

Chapter 7
Your Finances

"Money, like emotions, is something you must control to keep your life on the right track."
~ **Natasha Munson** ~

Unless you were born into wealth or married into it and have a never-ending source of income, you have to finance your retirement. Just as your parents financed your life when you were younger, and you have financed your life with your paycheck for the first half of your life, you must have a source of income to live your best second half of life! It is a sad scenario to get to a point in life where you have to choose between purchasing your much-needed medication and food. All too often, that is the situation of many older Americans. There is nothing wrong with being a store greeter, clerk, or whatever you choose to do in your latter years, but it should be from a place of having choices—not because your income does not cover all of your monthly expenses.

We typically start thinking about retirement very early in our working lives. We think about not having to get up to go to work every day or being able to do whatever we want. We even think about not working with or for people we consider less intelligent than we are. What we do not think about early on is how we are going to pay for those luxuries. Luxury is defined as "the state of great comfort that is often expensive." You have to be able to afford not having to get up early every day or being able to do what pleases you. You have to finance your retirement!

We are living longer than ever before in modern history. It is not uncommon to have octogenarians in our family, church, or community. So, God willing, if you retire at age 65, you may have another 25-30 years of living left. Unfortunately, Social Security has not kept up with the cost of living, so it will only replace a portion of your income when you retire. What do you do to get ready?

1. **Look at your current situation.** It is never too early nor too late to begin looking at your financial status. I am living proof that you cannot retire and live your best life if you are in debt up to your elbows. If you consider that your basic retirement income might consist of Social Security and a pension, it is safe to say you might have a monthly payment roughly reduced by two-thirds of your normal working income. That is barely enough to cover your mortgage and utilities. Begin to adjust your mindset regarding your spending habits. There is no way you can continue your existing spending habits when your income gets reduced drastically. If you are avoiding answering the phone to keep from talking to bill collectors now, think of what life will be like having to do that in your later years. Start to reduce your credit card debt now rather than later.

2. **Look at your income sources.** As with your working years, so it is with your retirement. You must have multiple streams of income. A little here and a little from there go a long way towards making your life more enjoyable. You never want to be in a position where you want or need something and have to say, "I'll have to wait until the 15th when my check comes in before I can do this." If you are living paycheck to paycheck now, you need to make some changes in your financial portfolio. That might mean getting a part-time job. There was a time when working a second job meant spending more time away from home and family, but today, many companies have "work from home" positions. Although saving money can be difficult, even small amounts will add up over a period of time. See if you can enroll in a savings program that will automatically deduct from your paycheck. Saying you will save it once it is in your hand is pretty unrealistic. The minimum financial situation upon retirement is Social Security and pension. The optimum should be those in addition to your savings, interest on investments, and a part-time job. It is never too late to start!

What do you want to do when you retire? How are you going to pay for it? If your plans are to downsize and live a quiet, modest life, your needs will be quite different than someone who still wants to maintain an active lifestyle. Most of us wait until after we retire and get bored before we think about what to do. Whatever you decide, it is going to cost you. Usually, those expenses are defined as "discretionary." That simply identifies the expenses as nonessential—meaning they are wants as opposed to needs. How are you planning to pay for them?

1. **Travel.** This goes without saying that you are going to need money to travel. Even if you plan on staying with relatives, you cannot go and expect someone else to finance your stay. You have to eat and will need transportation and entertainment costs.

2. **Remodeling your home.** Think of all those home improvement projects you have put off over the years because you just did not have the time. Well, now you have the time…but do you have the money? Even do-it-yourself projects can be costly. Before you start tearing down walls, you better figure out how to put another up in its place.

3. **Start a business.** Now that you are nearing the end of your career or have actually retired, it may be time to take the knowledge you have gained while working for someone else and convert it to your own business! Please note that starting your own business takes patience, drive, commitment, and (most of all) money. Even starting a nonprofit to work on something you are passionate about takes money to begin and maintain.

4. **Write a book.** How many times has someone said to you, "You need to write a book!"? There are very few of us who have come through life unscathed. Your journey—your testimony—might be the inspiration someone needs to get them through the challenges they

might be facing. As an author of five books, I can attest that writing the book is free, but it is just a diary if you write a bestseller and no one reads it. To get published — whether through a publishing company or by self-publishing — is not cheap.

Those are just a few examples of activities you can do while "living your best life." The common theme among them is the necessity of having the "discretionary funds" to accomplish the task. No funds, No fun!

So, how do you finance your life after the paychecks stop?

There are standard vehicles from which you can draw income after retirement, such as:
- An IRA
- A 401(k)
- A pension
- An annuity (or other life insurance product)
- Savings
- Social Security

As previously stated, we live longer, and it takes multiple income streams to support ourselves and enjoy what should be the best years of your life. Starting a plan for these should begin as early in your career as possible, but it is never too late to begin!

1. **Individual Retirement Account (IRA).** An Individual Retirement Account, or IRA (as it is more commonly

known), is a specialized investment account that you can open with any brokerage or bank. There are three categories of IRAs: Traditional, Roth, and Rollover. You can deposit lump sums into an IRA whenever you can or arrange automatic withdrawals from your checking account based on a monthly or annual plan. Depending on the type of IRA, you have different options for putting money into the account and what happens when you take money out. Traditional and Roth IRAs are contributory accounts that allow you to deposit money over a period of time. Traditional IRAs accept money only up to age 59 ½, and Roth IRAs accept money whenever you want to deposit it, no matter the age. The Rollover IRA is an account that does not accept contributions other than those in the form of a rollover. It receives money only from a former employer-sponsored plan, such as a 401(k) or another IRA.

Pros

Not employer-sponsored. Unlike a 401(k), an IRA is not dependent on your employer. As a result, the IRA is a popular retirement vehicle for full-time and part-time workers with no 401(k) option at work.

You get control. With an IRA, you get to decide where to open it, whether through a bank, mutual fund company, investment company, or online broker. Plus, you can choose your investment options within your IRA.

Cons

Lower contribution limits. Probably the biggest drawback to the IRA is its low maximum annual investment.

Contributions may not be deductible. For those with access to a workplace retirement account such as a 401(k), contributions to an IRA may not be deductible.

Roth IRA may not be available. Depending on your income and spouse's income, you may not be eligible to contribute to a Roth IRA.

2. **401(k).** A 401(k) is an employer-sponsored, tax-advantaged retirement account. Contributions to a traditional 401(k) reduce your taxable income on the front end, and the money in your 401(k) grows tax-deferred. You do not have to be traditionally employed to have a 401(k) account, but most people with a 401(k) are gainfully employed.

Pros

Higher contribution limits. For 2021, the contribution limit for employees who participate in a 401(k) plan is $19,500. Employees ages 50 or older can take advantage of catch-up contributions. In 2020, the IRS raised the limit on catch-up contributions by $500 to $6,500 from $6,000. This makes the 401(k) a great way to fund the majority of your retirement since even maxing out an IRA probably won't give you all the savings you need.

Possible employer matches or contributions. This varies from employer to employer. The best part for big savers is that your employer matches do not count towards your total contribution limit. So, you can contribute the maximum for the year, and your employer can kick in a matching contribution!

Borrowing capability. While rules vary, most 401(k) plans come with a provision that essentially lets you borrow from yourself. Typically, you can borrow up to $50,000 or half your 401(k) balance, whichever is less. This isn't always the smartest because you rarely pay yourself back. If you fall into real financial trouble, you may also be qualified for a penalty-free hardship withdrawal, which you will not have to pay back.

Easy to set up and make contributions. Most employers make it very easy to start saving for retirement. Contributions come directly from an employee's paycheck, and online access makes it easy to choose and change investment options.

Cons

Less flexibility. Since your employer chooses your 401(k) provider, you get less flexibility in terms of investment options. They may or may not have made a good choice to begin with, and you might not get many good investment options within your 401(k) account.

Possible waiting periods. If you start with a new employer, you may have to wait six months to a year before they will allow you to join their 401(k) plan. Unless you stash retirement savings elsewhere, that is a long period of missed retirement account contributions.

3. **Pension.** A pension plan contributes your money to a pool of funds that the plan owner then invests on your behalf. It is available predominately for those working in the public sector, large corporations, or the armed forces. Employer contributions to qualifying plans are tax-deductible; employee contributions and growth is tax-deferred until withdrawal.

    Pros

    Steady stream of income. This means income for the retiree and possibly their spouse for your entire life. It can protect you against the risk of longevity — the chance that you will live longer than expected and outlive your assets.

    Insulation from market fluctuations. Pension benefits are determined by factors that are not influenced by the market. Pensions are usually determined by your salary and years of service.

A certain level of comfort. A significant benefit is your comfort in being less dependent on your investment portfolio than those whose only source of income in retirement is Social Security.

Cons

A risk for beneficiaries. If you choose 100% survivor benefit, which will result in a lower monthly payout to you, your spouse may face loss of some income upon your demise. If you are single when you pass, the pension asset disappears completely without further benefit to your heirs.

Inflexibility of income. You cannot choose when you receive it. You cannot reduce current benefits (for tax purposes). Nor can you draw on future benefits (unless you borrow funds). For example, pension funds are not available to you to use for unexpected medical costs or any other lump sum expense.

4. **Social Security.** Social Security is a U.S. program that was signed into law in 1935. The goal of the program was to provide benefits to retirees. Any program like this has its fair share of pros and cons.

   Pros

   It provides a monthly income. This ensures retirees a guaranteed income during their retirement years. Although it is not a complete replacement, it does provide a supplemental income that can help individuals, couples, and families maintain their lifestyles.

It allows spouses to collect benefits. Although this program was designed to reward those in the workforce with a guaranteed income at retirement, non-working spouses are also eligible to collect benefits.

It allows you to continue working during your retirement. If you decide to keep working during your retirement, then you can potentially earn a larger benefit over time. That is because you will keep earning credits, if needed, to your advantage. Working can also delay the need to claim Social Security, which can increase the benefit as well.

It is a guaranteed lifetime income. Once your application for Social Security is approved, you are guaranteed a monthly benefit for the rest of your life. Even if you claim an early retirement, you will still receive that guaranteed check each month. That means you will have a substantial income you can rely on to meet your daily living needs each month. You can even invest this money if you choose.

Cons

The system is not fully funded. It is estimated that by 2028, the number of people claiming Social Security will exceed the number of people paying into it. The reality is that the money you put into this system was not put into an "account" waiting on you to claim your benefits. It was used to pay earlier retirees. Likewise, in order for you to collect your benefits, workers must continue to pay into the system.

It is not available to everyone. Under the existing Social Security program, you must earn a minimum of 40 credits to be eligible to collect benefits. To earn credits, under 2018 rules, you must make a minimum of $5,280 over a 12-month period for the maximum four credits allowed. That means it takes ten years to qualify for the minimum number of credits.

The full retirement age changes. People are living much longer than they were before the program was first introduced in 1935. For those born between 1943-1954, their full retirement age in the program is 66. The full retirement age for those born in 1937 or earlier is 65. For everyone born in 1960 or later, the full retirement age is 67. The program's retirement age keeps going up, so those born in 1980 or later may face a retirement age of 68 or older to make a "standard" claim for benefit, which would be three full years later than previous generations.

You cannot change your benefits. Although you can make a claim at age 62 for Social Security benefits, you will receive a 25% reduction in the overall benefit amount you would receive if you waited until your full retirement age. Any reductions in the benefit amount are permanent. If you lived to the age of 85 and made an early claim, you would actually receive less in benefit dollars than if you had waited until your normal retirement age.

Living your best life has to encompass a certain level of financial stability and security. You have to finance the rest of your life, just as your paycheck funded your working years. "If you are 55 and 'short on savings,' you'd better take drastic action to catch up while you are still employed and generating earnings," says John Frye, CFA, Chief Investment Officer of Crane Asset Management, LLC in Beverly Hills, California. "It's said that people's 50s (and early 60s) are their 'earning years,' when they have fewer expenses — the kids are gone, the house is either paid off or was bought at a low price years ago — and so they can put away more of their take-home pay."

So, get busy saving!

Living Your Best Life!

Chapter 8
Healthy Living

"If you can't fly, then run. If you can't run, then walk. If you can't walk, then crawl. But whatever you do, you have to keep moving forward."
~ Rev. Martin Luther King, Jr. ~

To most people, healthy living refers to both physical and mental wellbeing and that both are in balance and functioning well in a person. The World Health Organization (WHO) defines healthy living as "a state of complete physical, mental, and social wellbeing, not simply the absence of disease." Since we are mind, body, and spirit, our emotional wellbeing has to be considered and in sync in order for us to function within the parameters of "healthy living." All three of these states of being are so closely linked that when there is a change in one, it can cause a chain reaction and send all others out of kilter!

Let's look at an example of how physical, mental, and emotional states are connected:

You have a toothache (physical). The pain causes you to be bad-tempered (mental). You then lash out at your children for making too much noise (emotional).

Physical fitness is not the sole basis of being healthy. Being healthy means being mentally and emotionally fit as well. Being healthy should be a part of your overall lifestyle. Living a healthy lifestyle can help prevent chronic diseases and long-term illnesses. Feeling good about yourself and taking care of your health are important for your self-esteem and self-image. Maintain a healthy lifestyle by doing what is right for your body, mind, and spirit. You have to create a balanced life, which requires all aspects of yourself to work in harmony to create wellness.

Why is this so important? A healthy lifestyle is a valuable resource for reducing the incidence and impact of health problems, recovery, coping with life stressors, and improving quality of life. A growing body of scientific evidence shows our lifestyles play a huge part in how healthy we are. What we eat and drink, how much we exercise, whether we smoke or take drugs…all will affect our health in terms of life expectancy and how long we can expect to live without experiencing chronic disease.

Conditions such as heart disease, cancer, diabetes, joint disease, and mental illness are responsible for a vast number of deaths and disabilities. Currently, we rely almost exclusively on the provision of clinical care by highly-trained health professionals as our primary strategy to deal with those conditions. Many health problems can be prevented or at least their occurrence postponed by having a healthy lifestyle.

1. **Physical health.** Being physically active helps you look better, feel better, and live better! It is a proven fact that

staying physically active is one of the best ways to keep our bodies healthy and, therefore, live a better life.

   a. **It helps keep the doctor away.** It has been proven that too much sitting and other sedentary activities can increase your risk of heart disease and stroke.

   b. **It can help you live longer and better.** We are living longer. Now, the 70s have become the new 50s, but only if they're healthy. People who are physically active and at a healthy weight live about seven years longer than those who are not active and are obese.

   c. **It keeps you physically fit and able.** When you do not have regular activity, your body will eventually lose its stamina and strength. As we age, this becomes more and more evident. How long does it take you to get off the floor at 60 compared to when you were 30? Exercise increases muscle strength, which, in turn, increases your ability to do other physical activities.

   d. **It improves memory and brain function.** Physical activity can also indirectly enhance your memory and thinking by improving mood and sleep by reducing stress and anxiety. Problems in those areas frequently cause or contribute to cognitive impairment.

It's a busy life for most of us. Some say, "Life begins at 50!" Keeping ourselves healthy is all too rarely near the top of our list of 'things to do.' For some, it's not even on the list — or it's on the 'I should be exercising more' list. Convenience often wins. We are all so busy that convenience is at a premium. It is so important to make 'keeping healthy' a part of our day-to-day living habits. Living longer should not be our goal; living a longer, healthy life should be what we strive to do.

Your health depends on what you do throughout the day, every day. A healthy lifestyle is absolutely vital. Whatever your age, fitness level, or body shape, it is never too soon or too late to start thinking about living healthily. You can take a step towards healthy living by making one change now to your daily life.

2. **Mental health (joy and happiness).** People often confuse joy with happiness. Although they are closely related and often coincide, those emotions are not synonymous. Happiness is an emotion that brings intense pleasure, excitement, satisfaction and requires an external stimulus. Happiness occurs as a result of something or because of something. It is an outward expression. Joy, on the other hand, is an inner feeling. "Whereas happiness can be easily manufactured, joy comes through setting up the right conditions for it to suddenly appear," says Forrest Talley, Ph.D., a Clinical Psychologist in California. "Happiness can be brought about by a good cup of coffee in the morning or a funny movie. Joy is more difficult to cultivate." Joy is an

ongoing process that takes time. So, how can you find happiness vs. how to attain joy in your life?

   a. **Happiness.** Have you ever asked yourself, "What does happiness mean to me?" It might seem like a simple question, but happiness is relative. What makes you happy is probably not what someone would consider happiness to be. This would lend itself to the theory that happiness is largely dependent on an outward occurrence or stimuli. Your definition of happiness might be the perfect mate. To someone else, it might be a good job. Another might find happiness in a day of rest and relaxation. Very often, people focus on goal-oriented happiness. It is felt that once you achieve the desired outcome, you will be happy. But what happens if, for some unforeseen circumstance, you don't achieve that goal? Typically, you would become disappointed and unhappy. Although we don't hear of the term often, "self-happiness" is a sense of satisfaction and happiness with yourself. It is often associated with self-confidence, self-esteem, and, in general, it means you are pleased with yourself, your choices, and with the person you are. How do we get to that state of "self-happiness"?

      i. **Be in the moment.** Don't stress about things you have to do in the future or the "would'ves," "could'ves," or "should'ves" from the past. Focus on what you need to do right now to accomplish what you are trying to do.

ii. **Find resilience.** The scariest times are not when you feel overwhelmed or stressed. Rather, it is the feeling that you cannot pull yourself out of the dark hole that you sometimes find yourself in. Teach your brain how to calm down, relax, and bounce back or out of strenuous situations.

iii. **Manage your energy.** Don't get worked up over small things that won't matter in a short time. "Don't sweat the small stuff" is a powerful mantra. Manage your thoughts to focus on what is important. Wasting your mental capacity on people or thoughts that don't matter is the ultimate waste of your time.

iv. **Treat yourself well.** How you treat yourself is how others will treat you. No one should have more respect for you than yourself. Recognizing your faults with compassion and a willingness to improve makes you more likely to recover and move on from your mistakes.

Your happiness is your responsibility. Walk in the beauty and power of being authentically you. You are and have always been a whole and complete person. You do not need more things or people to be who you were created to be: HAPPY!

b. **Joy.** Joy is an emotion. Merriam-Webster defines emotion as "a conscious mental reaction; a state of feeling." Thusly defined, joy is an internal reaction. You can have joy from the simplest of situations, such as waking up in the morning to an intense situation, jumping for joy after winning a hard-fought competition, or doubling over in uncontrollable laughter when someone tells a hilarious story. We squeal with delight after getting a surprise gift and whoop and holler exuberantly when we hear fantastic news. For the majority of people, they live in a "me-centered" world. We tend to look at how people, things, and situations impact us. If we're not careful, we can become preoccupied with "me," "what I like," "what others think of me," and "why things aren't going my way." To experience pure joy, you must step outside of the "me" box and become a part of something much larger than you. How can you live a joyous life?

   i. **What are you passionate about?** If you are fortunate, you may discover your passion in the first half of your life. Even better, you may even get a chance to pursue it. But for most of us, we're too busy living our current lives, trying to be happy in the midst of taking care of our responsibilities to concentrate on anything else. That is why it's so vital that you discover what you are passionate about as you enter the next chapter of your life (which could be the best chapter). Retirement is no longer packing up, moving to Florida, and sipping tea or golfing all day. It is the time when you begin to work in your purpose—and your purpose is found within your passion. Again, I ask: What would you do, even if you weren't getting paid to do it? That is your passion! It is time to turn your passion into a profit!

ii. **Set goals.** Now, more than ever, is the time to set goals for yourself. For most of your life, your goals have centered around your life and livelihood—having a good job with good pay, keeping that good job, providing for your family, and (hopefully) going on vacation at least once a year. Now, your life is no longer centered around your livelihood. Instead, all of a sudden, you don't have structure. You are not required to get up at a specific time, be somewhere at a particular time, or stay anywhere longer than you wish to be there. So, what do you do? You set new goals! What do you want to be when you grow up? "There Is Life After…" Discover what that life looks like for you after 50 and/or after retirement.

iii. **Volunteer.** Believe it or not, there is so much joy in volunteering! When I finally stopped blaming other people for the chaos in my life, I ended the abusive relationship with myself. Trying to find me in the midst, I decided to volunteer at a women's domestic violence shelter. I intended to help the women at the shelter, but what ended up happening was the women helped me! Volunteering is a way to bring happiness to someone less fortunate and adds much joy to your life. There are so many causes you can bring your life skills and experience to that need people to help them. Most often, through volunteering, you ultimately will find your passion and, therefore, your purpose. There is no greater joy than walking in your purpose!

iv. **Seek out positive people.** People have a significant impact on your life. That being said, you should choose those you spend time with in the same manner you choose other important aspects of your life. Some people are considered to be parasites. They can suck the joy, happiness, and energy out of your life. You need to recognize those people and limit the amount of time you spend with them. Positive people should add value to your life, whether through thought, word, or deed. They enrich your life and inspire you to be a better person, motivate you to achieve your goals, empower you to make the changes you need to succeed, and cheer on your success.

3. **Emotional health.** Emotional health is also a very important part of your overall healthy living. It involves your ability to cope with both positive and negative emotions, along with having good coping mechanisms to deal with life's challenges and situations. Emotional health affects all aspects of your life, including your work, relationships, and overall health.

    a. **Peace of mind.** Peace of mind is described as "a mental state of calmness or tranquility; a freedom from worry and anxiety." Your state of mind is so important in a world full of stress and strain but is oftentimes very difficult to attain.

        i. Minimize the time you spend reading newspapers and watching the news. Most of it is negative.

        ii. Avoid negative people and negative conversations. Since peace is a positive mental state, negative input will destroy that.

    iii. Stay away from "messy" people — you know…the ones who keep stuff stirred up all the time.

b. **Laughter.** It's true! Laughter is strong medicine! It draws people together in ways that trigger healthy physical and emotional changes in the body.

    i. Laughter strengthens your immune system, boosts your mood, diminishes pain, and protects you from the damaging effects of stress. Nothing works faster or more dependably to bring your mind and body back into balance than a good laugh.

    ii. Humor lightens your burdens, inspires hope, connects you to others, and keeps you grounded, focused, and alert.

    iii. It also helps you release anger and forgive sooner.

c. **Your past.** We all have regrets — things in our past that we just hold onto. How often have you said or done something you wished you hadn't? Have you regretted putting dreams or goals on hold that went unfulfilled? We sometimes end up in situations that we didn't plan on. Throughout our lives, things "happen" that change our situations.

> i. What was the lesson you learned from your past? Life is about lessons and, if you don't learn the lesson, you will continue to repeat the behavior with the same results.
>
> ii. What's in your mental junk drawer? Have you ever said something and then thought, "Where did that come from?" It came from something you were holding onto that maybe you should release once and for all.
>
> iii. Don't let your past control your future. You must understand that you sabotage yourself by carrying baggage. Everybody has baggage they bring to the table. It's like a trunk full of stuff that you just continue to pile more things on top of. You don't even know what's at the bottom of the pile, yet you keep carrying it with you into the future.

d. **Gratitude.** "An Attitude of Gratitude!" Gratitude is thankfulness, being aware of your blessings, and acknowledging everything you receive. It shifts your life focus to the abundance in your life versus what you are lacking. Oprah once said, "Be thankful for what you have; you'll end up having more. If you concentrate on what you don't have, you'll never have enough!" Gratitude has a positive effect on your emotional wellbeing, personality, and overall health.

 i. **Emotional wellbeing.** If you are grateful for what you have, you feel better about your circumstances and yourself. Besides making you happier, gratitude enhances your positive emotions and increases your self-esteem.

 ii. **Personality.** Gratitude decreases your self-centeredness and promotes an attitude of giving. Your blessings come from giving, not receiving. You are also more likely to be less materialistic. When you become grateful for what you have, you become less fixated on getting more.

 iii. **Health.** In addition to promoting a balance in your emotions and relationships, an attitude of gratitude can also improve your physical health. In addition to reducing your depressive state and lowering your blood pressure, gratitude goes a long way in improving your sleep and overall health.

Being healthy should be a part of your overall lifestyle. Your self-esteem and self-image are all about feeling good about yourself and taking care of your health. Maintaining a healthy lifestyle is not that difficult and does not require a lot of work. What it does require is a concerted effort to… *Live Your Best Life!*

Chapter 9
Faith and Forgiveness

"Faith is unseen but felt. Faith is strength when we feel we have none. Faith is hope when all seems lost."
~ Catherine Pulsifer ~

"Forgive others, not because they deserve forgiveness, but because you deserve peace."
~ Jonathan Lockwood Huie ~

What is faith? Faith is defined as "complete trust or confidence in someone or something." The expression, "Just have faith," is used by people to encourage someone facing serious problems or stressful situations.

How strong is your faith? Who do you have faith in? In order to live your best life, you must have faith—not only in God but also in your fellow humankind. Let's look at both:

1. **Faith in God (or whoever your higher being is).** The Biblical definition of faith is "the substance or assurance of things we hope for but have not yet received." Faith (confidence, belief, trust) is also evidence of what is not

seen — the invisible spiritual things. Faith comes before a prayer is answered or before an individual has received what they have requested from God. If we have received what we asked for, then faith is not needed. Did you know there are different types of faith?

a. **Apathetic Faith.** This type of faith never takes root. It was planted, but because it was not grounded, it became weak. If we're not careful, our faith becomes a repetition of quotes, sayings, and verses. This can stem from familiarity, boredom, mediocrity, or just an overall disconnection. If you sense you're becoming apathetic in your faith, do something. Say yes to that thing you've been meaning to do or say no to that thing you really shouldn't be doing. Take one step to stir your soul to life to live your best life!

b. **Selfish Faith.** This type of faith is me-centered. Its belief is focused on the premise that if you pray enough, serve enough, and do enough good works, you will be richly blessed. You become so focused on seeing what you will get from what you are doing that when your actions don't result in the desired outcome, your faith soon withers and dies. We've all met someone who said, "I'll do for you, but what's in it for me?" A selfish kind of faith will never, ever lead you to your best life. When you become so concerned with yourself, that's where you'll end up — with just yourself!

c. **Material Faith.** This type of faith focuses on the creations, not the Creator. People who subscribe to this kind of faith become obsessed with their possessions. This can become apparent in many ways, such as buying a mansion, only to have the majority of rooms remain unused or buying bigger, flatter televisions that go unwatched or insisting on having the latest and greatest Apple product on the market soon as it is released. Our entire economic system loves those who buy, buy, buy! Everybody buy! It doesn't matter what you buy, just buy! Our entire civilization now rests on the assumption that no matter what else happens, we will all continue to buy lots and lots of things. We can become so enthralled with all of our "stuff," the thought of losing something becomes a terrifying ordeal. When you chase the next best, biggest, or latest "thing," you cannot live your best life!

d. **Devoted Faith.** This is a dedicated faith built to withstand the tests and trials of life. This is a faith that is centered on a higher being. For the Christian faith, that is Christ. Regardless of your faith—Muslim, Buddhist, Hindu, Catholic, or other—we all believe in a higher power that we entrust our faith in. This type of faith requires you to hold onto things that are yet unseen—a belief that things will work out if we just hold on and don't give up. Things are going to get better! Hold on! Don't quit! Live your best life!

Those explanations of faith require us to examine our own faith. Where do you fit with these? Are you happy about where your faith is currently? What motivates you and your faith? Once you fully recognize where your faith is, you can begin to fully realize where you are and where you're trying to go. Let your faith begin to lead you to your best life!

2. **Faith in man.** I don't know about you, but I've gotten to the point where I don't even look at the news anymore. These days, killings, bombings, kidnappings, and gun violence seem to dominate the news. Too much of that kind of news can make you feel hopeless and helpless. It can destroy your faith in your fellow man, although having faith in humanity is essential to living your best life. How is it possible to have faith in something you cannot see AND believe in the goodness in humanity? It's a proven fact that what you go looking for, you will ultimately find. So, if you intentionally look for the good, you will find it. Faith in humanity matters because it is the very thing that will heal what is broken in this world. Given the times we are in, it makes sense that some of us feel down and experience a sense of helplessness or dread. However, infusing inspiration into our lives could help us protect our own mental health while fighting for our moral values and adhering to doing what is right. So, how do we maintain faith in humankind?

   a. **Be intentional in your selection of news media.** Just because I don't look at the news doesn't mean I am not aware of what's going on in the world.

News generally focuses on sensationalism. A shooting, killing, or bombing. That is what sells and what news media outlets promote. Be intentional about seeking out good, positive news. It does your heart good to see someone helping another or hear of someone rescuing another from a dangerous and potentially fatal situation. Seek out those kinds of stories. If you don't know where to find them, simply Google "random acts of kindness." Tapping into those inspirational stories will help you live your best life by increasing your faith in humanity — especially when you see that kindness still exists in this world.

b. **Be intentional about what you post on Facebook and other social media outlets.** You may have a difference of opinion about something you see on Facebook, or someone might take issue with a comment you make. Arguing and going tit-for-tat might give you momentary relief, but the ensuing circumstances may cause you more emotional and mental distress than it's worth. Plus, at the end of the day, it's highly unlikely you will change anyone's mind. More importantly, don't follow "messy" people — the ones who always seem to keep stuff going or tend to spread unsubstantiated claims. The more you subscribe to that kind of madness, the more you will see those types of posts on your newsfeed. Instead, create and comment on positive, uplifting posts.

That way, you will see more of them and fewer negative, messy posts. I post an "Inspirational Thought" regularly on Facebook, and now, all I see are positive posts. See? What you put out there comes back to you! Live your best life on social media!

c. **Be intentional about volunteering.** Volunteering is good for your emotional, mental, and spiritual wellbeing. You can never hear "Thank you!" too often, especially when your help has made a difference in someone's life. While your volunteering efforts offer vital support to people in need, the benefits to you can be even greater. Giving to others can reduce stress, combat depression, keep you mentally stimulated, and provide you with a sense of purpose. It is impossible to live your best life without purpose! With our busy lives, it might seem an impossible task to find the time to volunteer, but doing so does not have to be a long-term commitment or take a tremendous amount of time out of your day. Giving in even the simplest ways can help someone in need and go a long way to improving your health and happiness.

It might be time to look at the faith you have in yourself as well. If you look at most of humanity and only see the negative, perhaps the problem lies within. Henry Miller once said, "The man who is forever disturbed about the condition of humanity either has no problems of his own or has refused to face them." If you've had a hard life, stop being hard on yourself. Learn to forgive yourself and believe in yourself more. Step out of your comfort zone to learn new things and push yourself to do something that you're worried you might fail at doing. Be bold! The world deserves your talents!

What is forgiveness? Forgiveness can mean different things to different people, but generally, it is "a conscious decision to let go of feelings of resentment and revenge." Everyone has been hurt by the actions or words of someone. Whether you were criticized by someone you love, your project was sabotaged by someone you trusted, or you've had a traumatic experience caused by someone close to you, we've all been there. Those wounds often leave you with lasting feelings of anger and bitterness. If you don't practice forgiveness, you will be the one who suffers.

Holding onto anger is like drinking poison and expecting the other person to die! While they go on with their lives—sometimes not knowing or even caring about the pain they've inflicted on you—you slowly deteriorate physically, mentally, and emotionally. The benefits of forgiveness far outweigh the consequences of nurturing that unforgiving spirit.

3. **Benefits.** Many people think that by forgiving someone, you admit that whatever happened wasn't that much of a big deal or that you absolve the person of any responsibility. In fact, forgiveness has nothing to do with the other person. Forgiveness is purely a selfish act of

cleansing yourself of all the negative baggage accompanying an unforgiving spirit. It allows you to:

a. Maintain healthier relationships.

b. Have less stress, anxiety, and hostility.

c. Build a stronger immune system and have a healthier heart.

d. Have improved self-esteem and lessen the chance of becoming depressed.

It's normal to want someone to regret the pain they caused you. Unfortunately, that does not always happen. Some people never recognize, or worse, don't care about your feelings. Letting that bitterness and resentment take up residence in your heart give them power over your life. Practicing forgiveness can help you find peace and joy to live your best life! To live your best life, take what you've learned and use it to protect yourself from future hurt.

4. **Effects of holding a grudge.** We hold onto grudges long after someone has done something to hurt us. Holding onto that grudge allows us to respond to the feeling that we've been wronged. It's an excuse for our "bad" behavior. That unforgiving spirit causes you to:

   a. Bring that anger and bitterness from your past into every new relationship or experience.

b. Become so focused on the wrongs of your past that you can't enjoy the benefits of your present.

c. Become depressed or so anxious that you lose valuable connections with others who could truly enrich your life.

d. Experience an out-of-balance life. It's impossible to find meaning and purpose in your present life if you have yet to turn the page from your past.

While it's important to process and work through grudges, holding onto those feelings is unhealthy and could have dire consequences, although rushing to forgive is often just as detrimental. Instead, take time to work through those complicated feelings. Get mad. Grieve. Wallow. Have a pity-party…for just a moment. You cannot let those feelings become a long-lasting state of being if you are aiming to live your best life!

5. **How do you reach that state of forgiveness?** When someone you trust hurts you, it may seem like you will never get over it. Even after your immediate anger passes, you may often hold onto the betrayal instead of letting it go so that it can fade into the recesses of your memory. To reach a state of forgiveness, you must realize what forgiveness is not. It doesn't mean you forget what happened, that the pain it caused is insignificant, or that you still have to interact with that person. Forgiveness simply means letting go of your anger, hurt, or desire for revenge.

a. **Acknowledge what happened and your feelings about the situation.** Don't pretend it didn't hurt. It did! It's okay to be angry. The problem comes when you hold onto that anger to the point it becomes detrimental to your health and wellbeing.

b. **Then, consider your role.** However much you might consider yourself the victim, if you search hard enough, you will discover the choices you made that might have aided in the betrayal. Were there signs you chose to ignore?

c. **Focus on the positive.** What did you learn from that experience? How can you prevent another such betrayal from happening? Life is about lessons. Until you learn the lesson, you will repeat it. In school, you learn the lesson then take the test. In life, you take the test and then learn the lesson!

Some people can easily forgive others, but for most, forgiveness takes some preparation and effort. Forgiveness is best regarded as an evolution rather than a one-time event. You may need to revisit the process repeatedly, but it should get easier each time. Eventually, you will realize your feelings about the other person's choices and behavior have changed in a deep and abiding way. That's when you will know you have learned to forgive for good and are on your way to living your best life!

6. **How do you forgive yourself?** While we might be willing to work on forgiving someone else, when it comes to forgiving ourselves, we tend to be much harder when it comes to releasing those feelings of anger and resentment. We all make mistakes, but learning from those bad choices, letting go, and moving on is vital to your overall wellbeing. It is impossible to live your best life if you are angry with yourself! Forgiving ourselves is a process, not a one-stop-shop!

    a. **Accept responsibility.** It is so easy for us to play the victim. "It wasn't my fault!" How many times have you heard that, or better yet, said it? Facing the choices you've made, what you've done, or what has happened is the first step in the process of self-forgiveness. Stop rationalizing or making excuses to justify your actions so that they become acceptable in your mind. Take responsibility and accept that you have made some bad decisions that may be the root of the consequences you are dealing with now.

    b. **Express remorse.** Once you have accepted responsibility, you will experience feelings of shame and guilt. When you've done something that requires forgiveness, it's normal—even healthy—to feel guilty about it. Those feelings are meant to serve as a springboard to positive behavior changes. While guilt suggests you're a good person who made a wrong decision, shame implies that you see yourself as a bad person.

Unresolved feelings of shame can lead to depression, addictive behaviors, or aggression. To live your best life, you must understand that making bad choices you feel guilty about does not make you a bad person or undermine your intrinsic value.

c. **Restore trust in yourself.** There is no one more important to trust than yourself. We can easily lose trust in ourselves after making a bad decision, and the consequences deem it necessary to forgive ourselves. Trusting yourself can build your confidence, make it easier to make decisions, and reduce your stress levels. The good news is that even if you don't trust yourself now, you can build that trust over time with some effort.

d. **Renew yourself.** Everyone makes mistakes and has things they're sorry for or regret. That's a part of life. But when you fall into the trap of rumination (which leads to a pity-party), that's where it can become damaging. There's nothing wrong with a pity-party. The problem is we don't know when to leave! A good 24-hour pity-party is a good thing—whether it's with chocolate, tears, or Jack. When the sun comes up, it's time to pick yourself up and figure out where you're going from there. You need to concentrate on the lessons to be learned so that you do not repeat the same behaviors.

Forgiving people who have hurt you can be challenging, but forgiving yourself can be even more difficult. It is important to remember that learning how to forgive yourself is not a one-size-fits-all process. It is never simple or easy, but working on this form of self-compassion has many mental, physical, and emotional benefits. In addition to reducing stress, depression, and anxiety, self-forgiveness can also positively affect your relationships.

Living Your Best Life!

Chapter 10
Finding Your Purpose

"The person without a purpose is like a ship without a rudder."
~ Thomas Carlyle ~

We spend our 20s trying to navigate life as we enter adulthood. Then, in our 30s, we're trying to figure out who we are and what we want. By the time we reach our 40s, reality begins to set in, and we start looking at our lives in terms of where we're going. We have stopped viewing ourselves through the lens of others and begin to search for a life with meaning and purpose.

We ask ourselves, "What is my purpose in life?" Usually, at that point, we are consumed with family, job, children, etc., and just dealing with the day-to-day situations of life. Those things don't leave much time for discovering our purpose! Suddenly, life takes on a deeper meaning.

Then, we approach our 50s. Our children are either getting ready to go off to college, already in college, or have started to forge their own path in life. At this point, I ask my clients, "What do you want to be when you grow up?" You are about to enter the next "Life After…" phase, and you have to think about what that will look like. By the time you are 50, you still have (hopefully) another 20-30 years of living left. How do you plan to spend that time? Will you travel, babysit your grandchildren, garden? Whatever you decide, if you don't have a purpose, it won't sustain you mentally, spiritually, or emotionally for the long haul.

That's why discovering your purpose becomes so important to living your best life. Having a sense of purpose impacts your health and helps you live a longer, healthier life. You are more hopeful about your future and can go with the flow more easily, not getting dragged down by challenging circumstances. You have better coping skills and a well-developed social support system to turn to when life's difficulties arise.

Finding your purpose is no easy task at this stage of life, especially if your purpose thus far has been centered on someone else's goals (i.e., your spouse, children, employer, etc.). You might struggle a bit in this, but remember: 50 PLUS is not the end of the road! Far more than any other generation, we reinvent ourselves, start new ventures, and pursue new opportunities. Your age is not your biggest hurdle, although if you are finding that you are stuck, the answer just may be how you feel about your age.

1. **Determine what you're passionate about.** Your purpose lies within your passion. What would you do even if you weren't getting paid to do it? Are people always raving about your cooking or your garden? Is there a cause or injustice that makes you scream or cry

every time you hear about it? Is there an issue you care deeply about but never got involved with because your life was too busy with kids, family, and job obligations? If yes, check it out now and see if you're still passionate about the subject.

2. **Start to volunteer your time and talents to something you want to support.** Having come out of a domestic violence marriage, I thought volunteering at a shelter would be a good thing. As it turned out, it was the best thing I could have done! Working with the women in the shelter helped me as much as it helped them. Offer your physical presence and your intellectual support to an organization to help them achieve their goals. Making a monetary donation is also an excellent way to get involved. Many causes rely on donations to keep doing the important work that is so needed. Whether through your physical presence, intellectual support, or monetary donation, get involved!

3. **Write down everything you're interested in.** Do you remember when you were little, and someone asked you, "What do you want to be when you grow up?" Write it down. When you put it on paper, it takes it out of your head (a thought) and becomes a plan (a goal). It takes on a life with meaning and provides an action plan when you can physically see it. Now, don't overthink it. Just one or two sentences will suffice. Keep your journal nearby and, as you think of more things, write them down, too. You will be surprised at some old dreams that may surface that you'd totally forgotten about!

4. **Consider your circle of friends.** Are the people you associate with positive and uplifting? Or do you spend more time complaining, criticizing, and talking about what you don't have, wish you had, or could have had? Many people are thriving and living their best lives after 50. If your circle of friends isn't encouraging and uplifting you, you don't have a circle…you have a cage! It will be next to impossible to discover your purpose within your passion if none of your friends are passionate about anything. Be careful not to become one of the "walking dead"!

5. **Network, Network, Network!** You have to meet new people. You have probably spent the last 20-30 years associating with the same people. Whether at work, your children's extracurricular activities, or the church community, it's likely been challenging to find the time to expand your network. Now is the time. Every city has networking events. It might be a book club or book signing. It could be an event that hosts a meet-and-greet. Or it could be a social club that has a common theme. Whatever it is, be creative in your search for like-minded people. Wherever I go, I'm telling people about my nonprofit that works with formerly incarcerated women to help them get their lives back on track. New people could help you learn about possible new interests that could translate into what becomes your life purpose.

6. **The perfect time is NOW to start doing something!** If you're sitting around waiting for your purpose to fall in your lap, you'll be sitting and waiting for a long time.

Try different things until something sparks your interest. Waiting is just another name for "procrastinating." Don't wait years because you're afraid to make a mistake or look foolish to those not on the same journey as you. DO SOMETHING! If you do nothing, nothing will get done. It's up to you to define your destiny and, in order to do that, you have to move off your couch!

7. **Set goals.** As we age, evolve, and change, so should our goals. That doesn't mean a goal you set for yourself in your past should be ignored. It does mean that we shouldn't spend all of our time lamenting over what we wished we had done. Now is the time to set new, realistic goals that excite and motivate you. Look at what you want to achieve, and then work your way backward to the present to see what steps you need to take on your new journey. Follow the S.M.A.R.T. goals formula: **S**pecific, **M**easurable, **A**ttainable, **R**elevant, and **T**ime-Bound.

8. **Never give up!** People think 50 PLUS is all downhill until we meet our Maker. Nothing could be further from the truth. Never in history has our demographics lived as long and had meaningful lives. Many are starting new careers after retiring. Retirement has taken on a new meaning. No longer are we retiring to sunny Florida. We are reinventing ourselves and remaining productive members of society. "Life After 50" begins a new chapter in our lives filled with excitement, joy, and happiness. Here's to living your best life!

Being 50 PLUS today means something totally different than it did for many of our parents and grandparents. It's not a time to give up and wait for the end of life. You're not at the beginning of the end; you're in the middle of the beginning! Finding a purpose in your life after 50 is figuring that out when you know yourself the best. It's a time when you have embraced who you are the most. Stop struggling with that and just embrace the possibility of living the life of meaning that you are created to live. You are FABULOUS!

Living Your Best Life!

Chapter 11
Scams, Slams, and Flim-Flams

"The fraudster's greatest liability is the certainty that the fraud is too clever to be detected."
~ Louis J. Freeh ~

According to research by the Stanford Center on Longevity and the Financial Industry Regulatory Authority's Investor Education Foundation, those over the age of 65 are more likely to have lost money due to a financial scam than someone in their 40s. To help the elderly avoid becoming victims of fraud scams, it is crucial to understand why they are targets, what schemes and tactics are commonly used against them, and how those schemes affect them.

1. **Why are seniors targeted?** Most victims of scams are seen as vulnerable, and, unfortunately, our senior population is perceived that way. Loneliness, a willingness to listen, and their trusting nature often attract frauds and schemers. They also usually have financial savings, own a home, and have good credit—all of which make them attractive to scammers. Additionally, seniors may be less inclined to report fraud because they don't know how or might be too

ashamed at having been scammed. They might also be concerned that their relatives will lose confidence in their ability to manage their own financial affairs. As well, when an elderly victim does report the crime, they may be unable to supply detailed information to investigators. With the elderly population growing and seniors racking up more than $3 billion in losses annually, elder fraud is likely to be a growing problem.

According to a recent study, people 50 and older hold 83% of America's wealth. Households headed by people in their 70s and 80s tend to have the highest median net worth. That makes them prime targets for financial scams—and the effects can be devastating. With an aging population, that is an elder justice issue, a personal finance issue, and a public policy issue. It's hard to pin down the numbers, but a study out of New York state estimates as few as one in 44 cases are ever reported. Studies have calculated that older people lose anywhere from $2.9 billion to $36 billion each year from financial exploitation.

2. **Scams targeting seniors.** Scammers use different tactics to get the elderly to fall victim to their schemes. In some cases, they can be friendly, sympathetic, and willing to help. Others use fear tactics. The tactic used generally depends on the type of situation the fraudster finds himself in with the elderly person.

   a. **Medicare.** In scams involving Medicare, fraudsters pose as Medicare representatives to get seniors to give them personal information such as their Medicare identification number. The fraudster uses that information to bill Medicare for fraudulent services and then pockets the money.

b. **Counterfeit prescription drugs.** As prices for prescription drugs increase, seniors turn to the internet to find lower prices for their medications. Unfortunately, fraudsters are aware of this and set up websites that advertise "cheap prescription drugs," which are usually counterfeit. Seniors who unknowingly purchase those counterfeit drugs soon realize they have been duped when the medicines do not provide any relief from their medical condition or even cause additional health problems.

c. **Funerals.** In one type of funeral scheme, fraudsters use obituaries to find out information about the deceased in attempts to extort money from family members or grieving spouses. They claim the deceased had an outstanding debt that must be paid immediately. Those close to the deceased are usually vulnerable and more likely to pay the fraudulent debt. In another scheme, dishonest funeral directors might try to deceive the elderly by capitalizing on their unfamiliarity of funeral costs and selling them unnecessary services such as a casket when the deceased is going to be cremated.

d. **Telephones.** Phone scams are the most common ones used against the elderly. Scammers might get seniors to wire or send them money by claiming to be a family member who is in trouble and needs money. They might also solicit money from the elderly by posing as a fake charity, especially after a natural disaster.

e. **Internet.** Since the elderly are usually not as savvy with handling emails and surfing the internet, they are easy targets for scammers. Victims have been tricked into downloading fake anti-virus software that allows scammers access to personal information on their computers. Seniors might also respond to phishing emails sent by scammers that ask them to update their bank or credit card information on a phony website.

f. **The 'Grandparent Scam.'** This scam is highly deceptive because it plays on the elderly's emotions. In a grandparent scam, a scammer calls an older person and pretends to be their grandchild. They ask them if they know who is calling, and when the grandparent guesses the name of one of their grandchildren, the scammer pretends to be that grandchild. The scammer then tells the grandparent they are in some sort of financial bind and asks if they can be sent money through Western Union or MoneyGram to help them out. The scammer also instructs the grandparent not to tell anyone about their "situation." Once the scammer receives the money, they often continue to contact the grandparent and asks for more money.

3. **How to avoid scams.** Whether it's online or over the phone, the following are some signs that you may be the target of a scammer:

    a. **A con artist may say…**

        i. You need to "act now," or the offer will expire.

        ii. You have won a free prize, but you need to pay for shipping and handling (or other fees).

        iii. You need to wire money or pay a debt with a gift card.

        iv. You need to handle payments (deposit funds for another person or forward money to someone else).

    b. **A fake website…**

        i. May appear as a pop-up in a new browser window.

ii. Will not display the secure lock by the web address at the top of the page.

   iii. Will look a little "off" or different from how it usually looks.

   iv. Will have bad reviews on Google or other search engines — or no reviews at all.

   v. May have typos or use bad English.

4. **How to protect yourself**

   a. **Tips for avoiding scams.** Anyone can become a target of fraud, no matter their age. But with careful research and smart decision-making, you don't have to be a victim.

      i. Take time to research whether companies, offers, and unexpected debts are legitimate. Have a loved one help you.

      ii. If a caller tells you to "act immediately" or does not give you time to research a company, they are probably a con artist.

      iii. Be wary of unsolicited emails and phone calls from companies and people.

iv. If something seems strange about a phone call, simply say, "No, thank you" — and hang up immediately.

v. Be careful of unusual emails or messages from family members. If a message contains a lot of typos or simply doesn't sound like your loved one, it may be a hacker.

vi. Make sure websites are secure before entering private information. Look for the image of a lock near the website's URL (address of the website).

vii. Remember: If something seems too good to be true, it probably is.

b. **Be aware.**

i. Recognize scam attempts and end all communication with the perpetrator.

ii. Search online for the contact information (name, email, phone number, address) and the proposed offer. Other people have likely posted information online about individuals and businesses trying to run scams.

iii. Resist the pressure to act quickly. Scammers create a sense of urgency to produce fear and lure victims into immediate action. Call the police immediately if you feel there is a danger to yourself or a loved one.

iv. Be cautious of unsolicited phone calls, mailings, and door-to-door service offers.

v. Never give or send any personal identifying information, money, jewelry, gift cards, or checks or wire information to unverified people or businesses.

vi. Make sure all computer anti-virus and security software and malware protections are up to date. Use reputable anti-virus software and firewalls.

vii. Disconnect from the internet and shut down your device if you see a pop-up message or locked screen. Perpetrators regularly use pop-ups to spread malicious programs. Enable pop-up blockers to avoid accidentally clicking on a pop-up.

viii. Be careful what you download. Never open an email attachment from someone you don't know. Be wary of email attachments forwarded to you.

ix. Take precautions to protect your identity if a criminal gains access to your device or account. Immediately contact your financial institutions to place protections on your accounts. Monitor the accounts and your personal information for suspicious activity.

5. **How to report.** If you believe you or someone you know may have been a victim of elder fraud, contact your local FBI field office or submit a tip online. You can also file a complaint with the FBI's Internet Crime Complaint Center. Each state also has a Division of Aging Services to assist the elderly. When reporting a scam—regardless of the dollar amount—include as many of the following details as possible:

   a. Name(s) of the scammer and/or company.

   b. Dates of contact.

   c. Methods of communication.

   d. Phone numbers, email addresses, mailing addresses, and websites used by the perpetrator.

   e. Methods of payment.

   f. Where you sent funds, including wire transfers and prepaid cards (provide financial institution names, account names, and account numbers).

g. Descriptions of your interactions with the scammer and the instructions you were given.

h. You are also encouraged to keep original documentation, emails, faxes, and logs of all communications.

Financial scams targeting seniors have become so prevalent that they're now considered "the crime of the 21st century." Financial scams often go unreported or can be difficult to prosecute, so they're considered a "low-risk" crime. However, they are devastating to too many older adults and can leave them in a very vulnerable position with little time to recoup their losses.

It's not just wealthy seniors who are targeted. Low-income older adults are also at risk of financial abuse, and it's not always strangers who perpetrate those crimes. Their own family members commit over 90% of all reported elder abuse — most often, their adult children, followed by grandchildren, nieces and nephews, and others.

We are living in some difficult times. Stay vigilant! Be aware! If your gut is telling you something isn't right, it probably isn't.

Living Your Best Life!

Chapter 12
The Sandwich Generation

"A hero is an ordinary individual who finds the strength to preserve and endure in spite of the overwhelming obstacles."
~ Christopher Reeve ~

Are you noticing that your caregiving obligations are filling up more and more of your calendar and to-do list? If you have found yourself drowning in both professional and family responsibilities, you aren't alone. In fact, many adults are in the middle of learning how to juggle caring for their children and helping out their aging parents. If you are trying to learn how to balance making it to your high schooler's basketball game and refilling your parent's prescription on the way, you are a member of "The Sandwich Generation."

As the elderly population grows and a new crop of young adults are financially struggling to attain a solid financial foothold in these trying economic times, individuals are 'sandwiched' between aging parents and adult children. You are often put in the position to care for both your children and parents simultaneously, and that support is often both emotional and financial. Hence, "The Sandwich Generation."

With people living longer, a new generation of caregivers has emerged. The "Club Sandwich Generation" is comprised of adults in their 50s or 60s who are responsible for the care of their aging parents, adult children, and sometimes grandchildren. In the Club Sandwich Generation, many are senior citizens themselves—people in their 60s and 70s taking care of parents in their 90s or older, while their children are old enough to have their own children. According to Tim Ross in *The Telegraph*, it's a clever name that recognizes the fact that there's a whole new layer—yet another generation added to the mix.

So, whether you are in your 50s, 60s, or even your 70s, you can be "sandwiched" between aging parents and children and/or grandchildren.

In 20 years, one in four families will include frail great-grandparents in their 80s and 90s, as well as infant great-grandchildren who will require childcare. Experts warned that the "squeezed" middle generation—aged 50 through 65—will face a double-whammy as they are asked to contribute towards the cost of educating and caring for their grandchildren and looking after their elderly parents. With more post-college young adults coming home to live with parents or doing so throughout school, there are now estimates that almost 30% of 25 to 34-year-olds reside with their parents. Essentially, that leaves parents to care for many of their children's financial burdens in addition to tending to other responsibilities that may accompany them.

As if that isn't stressful enough, if you are amid the sandwich generation, you are handed double-duty by also wanting or needing to help take care of your aging parents—a role many consider far more their responsibility than taking care of adult children. Whether your parents live in your home, in a facility, or within their own home, the stress can become overwhelming. The burdens of medical costs, helping with daily activities, overseeing supervision, legal considerations, and other concerns can take a physical and emotional toll on top of ongoing financial concerns.

With so many potential stressors, the sandwich generation can often experience:

- Caregiver burnout and feelings of depression, guilt, and isolation.
- Issues finding the time to be a good spouse, parent, and child simultaneously.
- Trouble managing work, hobbies, relationships, and "me-time."
- Psychological issues as they struggle with being pulled in multiple directions every day.

Caregiving as a member of the sandwich generation is both exhausting and expensive. A recent report by the Pew Research Center suggests that "more than 1 in 10 parents are caring for an adult in addition to their children." You can easily spend about three hours per day on caregiving duties that are split between your children and your parents. Juggling the emotional, logistical, and financial aspects is no easy feat, but there are ways to make the process easier.

1. **Enlist caregiving support.** Members of the sandwich generation are typically exhausted and in desperate need of some type of support from others. Tom Wilson, President of the Caregiver Partnership (a retailer for home health services and products), said, "Sandwichers typically aren't in the best frame of mind. We use three words: frantic, frazzled, and frustrated because they have no time and little money." So, what should you do? Wilson says, "If you are the primary caregiver, you need support." You shouldn't feel guilty about asking your siblings for help with costs, hands-on care, and spending time with your aging parent(s).

   But it's not always that simple, especially for women.

   The Family Caregiver Alliance reports that women provide unpaid, informal care that ranges from $148 billion to $188 billion annually. That amount of work can quickly translate to caregiver burnout, leaving family caregivers feeling exhausted, depressed, and even getting ill more often than their peers. Fortunately, if you can receive support from others, you will have the time for self-care, thus reducing your chances of feeling the effects of burnout.

   Caregiving tasks can be distributed and delegated among family members, including siblings. Tasks can also be provided by hired professionals to further lift the burden off the primary family caregiver.

If you are a primary family caregiver, don't be afraid or intimidated to ask for help. Often, you will find that your family, friends, and neighbors are ready to rally around you to provide the support you need. However, if you don't ask, your network will not have the chance to offer their help.

2. **Stay organized to avoid sandwich generation stress.** The seemingly nonstop demands on sandwich generation caregivers can be overwhelming. Staying organized can be helpful. Following are a few ways you can keep your caregiving tasks and support team on the same page:

    a. **Start by planning a monthly family meeting.** Talk about what's going on and what you need help with in the next month. You're more likely to get the help you need if you give very specific tasks. For example, ask if someone can pick up mom's prescriptions on the 1st and 15th of every month or if someone can drive dad to the doctor on specific days. Then, your family members can check their calendars and offer to take on those tasks. If there are any duties left over, you can enlist the assistance of community organizations or hired professionals.

    b. **Your regular meetings also allow you to set parameters so that everyone knows their responsibilities and your limitations as a dual-caregiver.** This will enable you to create a framework for communication and conflict resolution, which can benefit everyone while, at the same time, encourage the whole family to become a part of the caregiving plan.

c. **You can also harness technology to keep everyone on the same page concerning your parent's care.** Try a shared calendar or spreadsheet to keep track of doctors' notes, appointments, and health updates. You can also use apps such as MealTrain to organize meal drop-offs or other caregiver apps that can assist with organization.

3. **Prepare for financial challenges that face adult caregivers.** Dual-caregiving can be expensive. While secondary insurance can cover some expenses, bills can quickly add up. Check with a local office on aging or visit the National Council on Aging's Benefits Checkup site to find out what benefits are available. Some programs cover a wide range of needs, from nutrition to financial assistance with heating and cooling bills.

Stressing out about finances is common when caring for an aging parent, but you can feel more confident by being as proactive as possible. For example, involve your loved one's financial advisor in conversations about budget goals and milestones. You can also speak candidly with your parent's physician as you attempt to understand what challenges could arise in the near and distant future. That information will allow you and your family members to develop a timeline that can assist with financial planning.

Finally, you can also investigate ways to save even more money, such as setting up recurring prescription deliveries or utilizing Meals on Wheels.

4. **Get the support you need as a sandwich generation caregiver.** It's not easy being pulled in several different directions. However, don't let your caregiving duties prevent you from spending meaningful time with your parent. Many family caregivers often lose themselves in the caregiving role and end up missing out on the opportunity to relish in their daughter or son relationship.

   Carve out one visit regularly where you leave all caregiving duties such as refilling the pillbox or checking on the food in the fridge, at the door. Instead, spend that visit taking a walk, looking through a photo album, reading a book, or doing something special together. You will find those visits leave you feeling refreshed and ready to take on your busy calendar with more vigor and energy.

Remember: You don't have to handle your caregiving role alone. Even if you don't have an extensive support system, there are professionals available to step in and assist you and your loved one when you need it. If you're worried about your parent and whether they're thriving at home on their own, it's never too early to bring up the topic of senior living.

Living Your Best Life!

Conclusion

As human beings, one of our deepest-rooted desires is to have a meaningful and happy existence. You've probably heard the saying, "Live your best life," before. It's good advice!

We all want to feel connected to both ourselves and others. We want to feel that we're part of something meaningful and that we're making a difference in the world. We want to look back at our lives and achievements and be proud. In short, we want what the saying says: to live our best lives!

But what does it really mean to live your best life?

You are a unique individual, so living your best life is exclusive to you. Your best life will reflect your true values. It will be made up of what makes you happy and will be colored by what *making a difference* means to you.

Live each day like it counts, and remember: It is your choice. Your best life is unique to you, so don't compare yourself to others. Instead, focus solely on living your best life while enjoying the learning, exploration, and experiences along the way.

Be Blessed!

Living Your Best Life!

About the Author

Linda H. Williams has been homeless, an alcoholic, a victim of domestic violence, and hopeless. Everyone has a past. That was her past. Linda is now a Bestselling Author, Insight & Wisdom Coach, Facilitator, Speaker, and CAMS. Living your best life has to be intentional. *"I was well into my fifties before I even realized there was a better life,"* says Linda. Now in her seventies, Linda uses her gifts and talents to empower and encourage others to release the chains of their past in order to live their best lives.

She provides CBT-based life skills classes to local prisons and rehab programs. She also offers re-entry resources to formerly incarcerated women.

Linda is the author of several publications, including "Your Past Has Passed," "There Is Life After...," "Real Talk with Real People," and a journal entitled "Inspirational Thoughts..."

She holds a degree in English, is a Certified Insight & Wisdom Coach, a Cognitive Behavior Therapy Practitioner, and a Certified Anger Management Specialist.

Linda's "50 PLUS" mantra is:

"I am living my best life on purpose and with intention."

www.ingramcontent.com/pod-product-compliance
Lightning Source LLC
LaVergne TN
LVHW051842080426
835512LV00018B/3017